Also by Jay McGraw

Life Strategies for Teens

LIFE STRATEGIES FOR TEENS WORKBOOK

EXERCISES AND SELF-TESTS TO HELP YOU CHANGE YOUR LIFE

Jay McGraw

A Fireside Book
Published by Simon & Schuster
New York   London   Toronto   Sydney   Singapore

FIRESIDE

Rockefeller Center

1230 Avenue of the Americas

New York, NY 10020

Copyright © 2001 by Jay McGraw

All rights reserved,

including the right of reproduction

in whole or in part in any form.

FIRESIDE and colophon are registered trademarks

of Simon & Schuster, Inc.

For information about special discounts for bulk purchases,

please contact Simon & Schuster Special Sales:

1-800-456-6798 or business@simonandschuster.com

Designed by Interrobang Design Studio

Manufactured in the United States of America

10 9 8 7 6 5 4 3 2 1

Library of Congress Cataloging-in-Publication Data is available.

ISBN 0-7432-2470-1

CONTENTS

ABOUT THIS WORKBOOK

*E*VERY TEENAGER I HAVE EVER KNOWN WANTS TO BE HAPPY, self-confident, popular, and successful. We are willing to do just about anything in order to obtain these goals—we'll let other people make decisions for us, we'll do things against our own best judgment, we'll spend countless hours creating the "look" we think will get the right response. We'll trade our own individualities for the mere chance of being accepted, of being considered "cool." We'll do risky things we know could cause us a lot of trouble. We'll avoid trying something new in order not to face the possibility of ridicule or failure. We'll pass up the opportunity for new and interesting relationships or activities based on other peoples' ideas of what and who is cool or uncool. Living in a rut is a lot of work!

But making good decisions for yourself is also difficult if you don't know what you're after in life. How can you improve your life if you don't know what you want? Understanding what you want in life (what would make you feel happy, self-confident, popular, and successful) is at the core of the Ten Life Laws, the key to unlocking all of the doors that stand between you and what you'd like your life to be. It's going to take some work on your part to first figure out exactly how you'd like to improve your life and then take action to make it happen. You're going to have to be brutally honest with yourself, face some of the bad parts of who you are, and take a long, hard look at your choices, behavior, attitudes, and relationships.

The good news is, you've already taken the first step toward making big improvements by acquiring *Life Strategies for Teens* and this companion workbook. Make a promise to yourself to put them to work for you, to get as much out of them as you can. Then do the work; the exercises and assignments that follow will help you take a look at everything in your life based on whether it's working or not and whether you are getting the results you want or the results you don't want.

These books can't change you. You have to change yourself—and this book can help you do just that. However, your willingness to change must be there. Make that your second promise to yourself. I can't promise you that every problem in your life is going to disappear, or that every dream you have will come true. But I can assure you that if you do the work, you will become a stronger, wiser, and more competent person.

The purpose of studying the Ten Life Laws and putting them to work for you is to get what you want out of life. You already have within you all of the tools and talents you need to create a better, more fulfilling life; all that's left is for you to really *want* it.

LIFE STRATEGIES FOR TEENS WORKBOOK

PART I

WAKE UP!
Get Real with Yourself

BEFORE YOU BEGIN THIS PORTION OF **LIFE STRATEGIES FOR TEENS WORKBOOK**, READ THE **INTRODUCTION** THROUGH **POWERING UP** SECTIONS OF **LIFE STRATEGIES FOR TEENS.**

*T*O UNDERSTAND HOW TO GO ABOUT IMPROVING YOUR LIFE, the first thing you must do is figure out what isn't working and why. The material in this section of the workbook is designed to help you see your life clearly, to understand what the problems are, what you need to fix, change, get rid of, etc. You're going to have to take a seriously unflinching, honest look at yourself and the way you live in order to understand how you've gotten to where you are today. Be prepared to get into some topics that might make you squirm a little—you're going to realize the benefits, believe me.

You will have to do some writing in this workbook as well (hey, this is your story, I can't be expected to do it all). Putting your thoughts, observations, ideas, and dreams in writing helps you get outside of your own head in order to figure out what's going on inside it. Committing things to writing also makes them more real and more urgent—it forces you to really think a subject through and to be honest in your thinking. Please give all these exercises your best effort. You'll be doing yourself a major favor if you put in the time and energy here and now. So, let's get ourselves started.

A QUICK SELF-CHECK

Bring yourself up to date on your life so far; think of this as a trip to the mechanic. Chances are, you already have a pretty good idea of what the big, ugly problems in your life are. Read the following list and put a check mark beside any item that describes you right now. In the blank spaces provided, add any item(s) that you know you need to deal with right away.

_____ I have zero control over my life.

_____ My parents don't understand my life.

_____ My friends are two-faced and we frequently do not get along.

_____ I am hurt by the cliques that don't include me.

_____ I am tired of my peers trying to get me to do things that I don't want to do.

_____ I am surrounded by hypocritical adults and I don't trust them.

_____ I have no money and no way to get money.

_____ I have no transportation.

_____ I am feeling confused about what I want to become in life.

_____ I feel anxiety and pressure over grades and academic performance.

_____ I suffer from a lack of confidence.

_____ I feel I lead a lazy lifestyle.

THE STORY OF MY LIFE

So, you see that some elements of your life could really use some attention. Before you figure out just what to do, you should really take a stab at understanding how you got to this point in the first place. Make a timeline for yourself like the one that follows. Go back at least five years from now and note all of the *important* events, ones that were a big deal—family-related things, friendships beginning or ending, accomplishments at school or at another venue (sports, dance, drama, etc.). Place all of the positive events in boxes above the timeline and all the negative events in boxes below the timeline. You'll be amazed at the life-altering events you've forgotten about, or never considered as being really important, until you sat down and started thinking about them. Let's see what circumstances have led right up to this second in your life. . . .

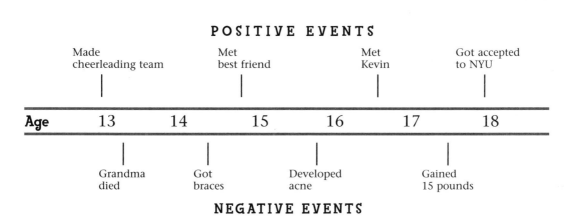

SAMPLE TIMELINE

POSITIVE EVENTS

Made cheerleading team		Met best friend		Met Kevin		Got accepted to NYU

Age	13	14	15	16	17	18

	Grandma died		Got braces		Developed acne		Gained 15 pounds

NEGATIVE EVENTS

Now write a short history. Tell it as if you were sharing it with a trusted friend, someone you could tell your deepest secrets to. Here are some examples of elements you can include in your story:

★ Significant childhood memories
★ Your relationships with your friends and classmates over the years
★ Your first big achievement or your first major disappointment
★ Main events in your home life
★ Main events in your school experience (academic/extracurricular)

Make it clear in your little memoir how you *felt* about all these events, people, and situations. If you felt happiness or pride, say so. If you felt sadness, pain, or guilt, say so. If you believe an event was so important that it changed the course of your life, say that too. This is your chance to get your past, your history, off your chest and into the great wide open of your journal.

WHY, OH, WHY?

If you're like everyone I know (myself included), you've made some really stupid decisions at one point or another—decisions that made you really hate your actions, if not yourself. Did you cheat on an exam and get caught and punished? Did you leave your little brother alone when you were supposed to be babysitting and something bad happened? Did you wear out your parents' patience by getting caught one too many times sneaking in after curfew? Did you lie to one of your friends and lose his or her trust? Did you get kicked off the team for some reason?

List five such scenarios in the following space. Provide some details: What prompted you to make the decisions you made, what were you hoping would happen, what is it about this situation that you would never again repeat? This is your chance to review the top five painful lessons you've learned about how *not* to live, what you *don't* want to be part of your life.

1. ....

....

....

....

2. ....

....

....

....

3. ....
....
....
....

4. ....
....
....
....

5. ....
....
....
....

START THINKING ABOUT WHAT YOU WANT IN LIFE

Before you go any further, consider this: Many of us have just stopped dreaming, stopped thinking of all things we can do and be, and now simply respond to what's happening in our day-to-day lives. Here's the reason for this problem: If you have no idea what you want, what your life should or shouldn't include, it is almost impossible to make any kind of plan for the future or to live with any kind of purpose. You have got to start wanting more excitement in your life, and to do that well, you must figure out what it is that will make you happy.

Remember when every week it seemed you wanted to be something else—a doctor, a fireman, a ballerina? Are you now out of touch with that desire to dream? If so, you need to start thinking about what you want to be and how you want to get there. The easiest way to identify the qualities you want in your life is to identify in others those qualities you would like to develop for yourself. This will help you put your finger on the very traits you'd like to encourage in yourself, that way you'll know what it is you'll be working for. The *how* will come later. Right now you need to get to know yourself a little better, and that is what this exercise will help you do. Really think about your answers and, as with all the activities in this workbook, have fun with them!

MY POSSIBILITIES

1. If you could choose any one person (famous or unknown, dead or living) to spend twenty-four hours with, who would he or she be? *Why* would you choose to spend a whole day with this person?

....

....

....

....

2. What are the qualities that you admire most in this person?

....

....

....

....

3. Which of these qualities would you like other people to mention when they

describe you?

....

....

....

....

4. Which, if any, of these qualities do you feel are already obvious in the way you live

your life?

....

....

....

....

5. For a few moments, imagine yourself developing the qualities you admire but don't feel you exhibit right now. How do you feel?

....

....

....

....

6. What are three concrete suggestions for actually acquiring just one of these qualities? What three things can you do, starting today, to become more like the person you admire so much?

....

....

....

....

BE WILLING TO TAKE POSITIVE RISKS

As I said in the introduction to this workbook, you must be willing to change. We know this is not as easy as it sounds, right? Isn't it funny how adults always remind each other and us that teenagehood is a period of experimentation, yet experimenting is the one thing they beg us not to do? The thing is, there are really two types of experimentation. The first type you probably know quite well, either first- or secondhand: smoking, drugs, alcohol, sex. But when it comes to the second kind of experimentation—taking a real chance that can actually create important, meaningful change in your life—we all have a tendency to back away, to become as afraid of this type of "experimenting" as our parents are of the other. Instead of taking a risk to improve the quality of your life, you settle for underachievement. You're afraid of failure, of being judged. Think of all the excuses you've used when you've debated with yourself about making a change. Put a check mark in the space next to any of the following excuses that have run through your head at one time or another. Beneath each excuse, indicate in a few words what risk you were thinking of taking when that excuse popped into your head. At the bottom of the list, add five more excuses from your personal greatest hits list.

☐ "I'm not doing that bad."

....

....

☐ "I am not old enough to worry about that yet."

....

....

☐ "Hey, my classmates have just as many problems."

....

....

☐ "I'm too busy with sports, school, or my hobby."

....

....

☐ "If I change, the friends I have won't like me anymore."

....

....

☐ "I'm doing as well as half the class."

....

....

☐ "Everybody who has pressured me to be different will think they have won."

....

....

☐ "I'm trying, but it's so hard."

....

....

☐ "Well, this is just how I am."

....

....

....

....

....

....

....

....

Keep in mind the words of hockey legend Wayne Gretsky: "You miss 100 percent of the shots you never take." It's the same way with life. If you want to be outstanding, no matter what you want to do, you must always take a shot. That means pushing yourself to make changes, to do better, know more, try new things, open up to new people, develop new skills—let go of what makes you feel comfortable! If you take this one risk, you may discover that the only person who is really holding you back is none other than yourself.

BEHAVIORS AND CONSEQUENCES

It is time to take off the blinders you've been wearing and recognize the negative behaviors in your life that have kept you from realizing your full potential—denial, inertia (laziness), and fear of failure. For example, maybe you spend your nights watching TV instead of studying for tests that you have to take the next day, even though you know that you need to get good grades on those tests in order to keep your GPA high enough to get into college next year. Maybe you sneak out of the house to go to parties where you drink alcohol, even though you know that if you get caught, you won't be going on the spring break trip you've been looking forward to for months.

In the next exercise, come up with ten events or outcomes in your life that you did not want, but helped to cause, and record them in the space provided. As you review these ten negative events or outcomes, take a brave look at how you contributed to setting yourself up for the results.

1. **EVENT:** ....

    Choices: ....

....

....

2. **EVENT:** ....

    Choices: ....

....

3. EVENT: ....

Choices: ....

....

....

4. EVENT: ....

Choices: ....

....

....

5. EVENT: ....

Choices: ....

....

....

6. EVENT: ....

Choices: ....

....

....

7. **EVENT**: ....

   Choices: ....

   ....

   ....

8. **EVENT**: ....

   Choices: ....

   ....

   ....

9. **EVENT**: ....

   Choices: ....

   ....

   ....

10. **EVENT**: ....

    Choices: ....

    ....

    ....

I am sure by now it is clear that in each of these negative events, you had some ownership in the problem. You have ownership because all of your choices and actions influence the events around you. Positive choices and actions have a positive influence on your experience; negative choices and actions have a negative influence. Just remember that in every aspect of your life, when you choose your behaviors, at the same time you choose the consequences of those behaviors.

WHAT'S *REALLY NOT* WORKING?

Give these questions your best shot. Be honest! If you admit to what isn't working in your life, you can come up with goals and strategies to change it.

What disturbs you about yourself? Make a list and be specific! For example: "I hate that I cave in every time someone pressures me into behavior I'm not ready for, like drugs, alcohol, or sex." "I hate that I eat even when I'm not hungry." "I hate the way I giggle when I'm nervous." "I hate that I can't get along with my parents."

....

....

....

....

What disturbs you about your life? Again, the more specific you are, the more helpful this list will be as you create your goals and strategies. You might say: "I hate the way my parents order me around." "I hate the fact that nobody at school will treat me the way I'd like them to." "I hate the way my clothes look on me." "I hate not having money of my own."

....

....

....

....

WHAT *IS* WORKING?

Look over your timeline and history again. What are ten really good things that have happened in your life—ten positive events or results—and what good choices did you make to help contribute to them?

1. **EVENT:** ....

   Choices: ....

....

....

2. **EVENT:** ....

   Choices: ....

....

....

3. EVENT: ....

    Choices: ....

....

....

4. EVENT: ....

    Choices: ....

....

....

5. EVENT: ....

    Choices: ....

....

....

6. EVENT: ....

    Choices: ....

....

....

7. EVENT: ....

   Choices: ....

   ....

   ....

8. EVENT: ....

   Choices: ....

   ....

   ....

9. EVENT: ....

   Choices: ....

   ....

   ....

10. EVENT: ....

   Choices: ....

   ....

   ....

Again, remember that when you choose your behaviors, you choose your consequences. And positive behaviors lead to positive consequences.

Based on the preceding list, what are five complimentary words or phrases you can write about yourself?

1. ....

....

....

2. ....

....

....

3. ....

....

....

4. ....

....

....

5. ....

....

....

These qualities that you appreciate about yourself are important. They form the basis of how you want to live in the future, and they will be the center of your strategy for life. It is only with your strengths and some serious hard work that you can overcome life challenges, particularly those you create for yourself. We can't forget that both mistakes and successes have something to teach us. Learn from your successes and remember the behaviors and attitudes that led to them. Remember so that you can repeat them in the future.

PART II

WISEN UP!
Understanding the Ten Life Laws

BEFORE YOU BEGIN THIS PORTION OF
LIFE STRATEGIES FOR TEENS WORKBOOK,
READ **LIFE LAW 1** THROUGH **LIFE LAW 10** IN
LIFE STRATEGIES FOR TEENS.

*E*VERY ASPECT OF YOUR LIFE IS GOVERNED BY A SYSTEM, A SYSTEM made of rules and restrictions, requirements and suggestions. When you are dealing with this system, knowledge is power. It is powerful because if you know the system, you can work with it and use it to get more of what you want. This next section of the workbook is designed to help you better understand the Ten Life Laws and how you can apply them to your life in order to better work with the system.

Be honest and thorough as you work through the following exercises. This workbook should be like a mental punching bag, you need to give it all you've got because it's not going to help you otherwise (likewise, you don't have to worry about it punching you back). As you would with a journal, use this book to unload, let down your guard, and give up the hidden truths of your life. Your reward will be as great as the effort you put into the process. What you need to do now is figure out what has gone wrong in your life and decide how to fix what isn't working.

LIFE LAW ONE
YOU EITHER GET IT, OR YOU DON'T

Your Objective: Become one who gets it. Understand what makes people tick—the basics of human nature. Figure out why you do what you do and learn how to change it.

Let's face it: Some people in this world are more successful than others. Whether it's the straight-A student, the captain of the football team, or the fantastic dancer, there are just some who live their lives one step ahead of the rest of us. They don't simply go out there and do okay, they do "great," "wonderful," "perfect." Is it because they are, in fact, perfect? Hardly! All of these people wake up in the morning with the same doubts, fears, and nagging insecurities as the rest of us. Actually, they are far from perfect. However, these people "get it." They understand that if you hold on to all the doubts and fears you wake up with, you'll never get out of bed. They know that in order to make it in this world, you've got to work for it. You've got to learn the system and then make the most out of it. That means saying no to the Saturday night party when there's work to do, it means being honest with your parents so they trust you when you're away at football games, it means having a job so you can afford those pricey dance lessons. Learning to work the system is far from difficult—it's all about avoiding what's going to cause more obstacles and breaking down the ones that are already there. By giving in to what's only going to hold you back, you jeopardize your dreams and your chances for success.

As you work through the following exercises, be prepared to look at what is holding you back, what parts of you are refusing to get with the system, and what actions or nonactions you are taking that stop you from being your best.

WORKING THE SYSTEM

Think about the people you know who are successful. Here's an example: Someone who "gets it" knows that getting good grades helps create a high level of respect and trust from parents and teachers. This person also knows that good grades lead to freedom and more responsibility in life. He or she accepts this fact and uses it to his or her advantage. When you are one of those who "gets it," you are the star in the movie of your own life. You are making things happen rather than waiting for them to happen. To get anywhere in life, you must first figure out where you want to go; the destination is not going to come to you.

A. Name three people (peers) that you admire who have achieved something you would like to achieve (good grades, a high level of skill in sports, music, or dance). Identify the achievement next to the person's name. Then, in the blanks, list five ways in which this person works the system to his or her advantage. (Example: Mary asked one of the older softball players to help coach her when she first got to school. By tryouts, she was not only a better player, but had come to know the team and the coaches.)

1. NAME: .... ACHIEVEMENT: ....

   a. ....

   b. ....

   c. ....

   d. ....

   e. ....

2. NAME: .... ACHIEVEMENT: ....

   a. ....

   b. ....

   c. ....

   d. ....

   e. ....

3. NAME: .... ACHIEVEMENT: ....

   a. ....

   b. ....

   c. ....

d. ....

e. ....

B. Think of the five skills, talents, or qualities you'd like most to develop in yourself. For each one, list five specific actions you can take in order to acquire the skill or nurture the talent or quality. How can *you* work the system? Your examples can be simple, such as improving your test scores in trigonometry, or more ambitious, such as landing a starting position on the varsity team next season. Or perhaps you'd like to put your naturally outgoing personality to work in order to widen your circle of friends.

1. Skill, talent, or quality: ....

a. ....

b. ....

c. ....

d. ....

e. ....

2. Skill, talent, or quality: ....

a. ....

b. ....

c. ....

d. ....

e. ....

3. Skill, talent, or quality: ....

a. ....

b. ....

c. ....

d. ....

e. ....

4. Skill, talent, or quality: ....

a. ....

b. ....

c. ....

d. ....

e. ....

5. Skill, talent, or quality: ....

   a. ....

   b. ....

   c. ....

   d. ....

   e. ....

Relationships run according to a system as well. You have to "get it" about people, too. Think about your relationships at school with friends, classmates, and teachers. Think about five ways in which you'd like your relationships *in general* to improve (e.g. "I'd like to get to know more people and have more friends than I do now," or "I'd like to stop being rude or cold to unpopular classmates the way my friends are"). Below each statement, list three *specific* actions you can take to make it a reality.

1. I'd like to: ....

   a. ....

   b. ....

   c. ....

2. I'd like to: ....

   a. ....

   b. ....

   c. ....

3. I'd like to: ....

   a. ....

   b. ....

   c. ....

4. I'd like to: ....

   a. ....

   b. ....

   c. ....

5. I'd like to: ....

   a. ....

   b. ....

   c. ....

Now think about your relationships with your parents, stepparents, brothers, sisters, and grandparents. Consider the annoyances, frustrations, and even hurt you cause one another. How can you improve your relationships so that everyone will be happier and you will get what you want (more independence, your parents' trust, your siblings' support, etc.)? For each of the five statements about how you'd like your interaction to improve, make three specific suggestions of ways in which you can make that happen.

1. IMPROVEMENT:

a. ....

b. ....

c. ....

2. IMPROVEMENT:

a. ....

b. ....

c. ....

3. IMPROVEMENT:

a. ....

b. ....

c. ....

4. IMPROVEMENT:

a. ....

b. ....

c. ....

5. IMPROVEMENT:

a. ....

b. ....

c. ....

WHAT MAKES US TICK?

To get anywhere in life, you must have some idea of what other people feel, experience, and desire—you must be able to understand what motivates the decisions they make (which aren't so different from your own, most of the time). If you take the time to figure out what matters to someone else, you'll know what you have to offer them. You will know what you can give them so that they will give you what you want. Learning more about how other people think—their views, backgrounds, and beliefs—can only help you throughout life. Observing others closely will also enable you to learn from those who "get it" (and those who don't). Think of three people you are close to and answer the following questions about each person. It may be that you are unable to answer some of the questions until you pay more attention to the person's behavior.

NAME: ....

1. What is most important to this person (for example, grades, popularity, sports, friends, family, kindness, generosity, or doing the right thing)? List the top five things in order of their importance to him or her.

....

....

....

2. Does this person have any significant fears, phobias, or hang-ups? Identify five specific examples.

....

....

....

3. Is he or she prejudiced about anything? Give three examples.

....

....

....

4. What qualities is this person drawn to in other people (friends, significant others, etc.)?

....

....

....

5. What qualities are you most drawn to in this person?

....

....

....

6. How does this person feel about him- or herself physically, intellectually, and socially?

....

....

....

7. What do you think this person wants most in his or her life?

....

....

....

Now see if you can go to each of these three people and ask them the questions out loud, or watch them closely and pay attention to these things. How accurate are your answers according to what these people say about themselves, or according to what you've observed?

What if *you* are the person you're observing? How would *you* answer a similar set of questions?

1. **What do you value most in your life? List the top three things in order of importance to you.**

....

....

....

2. **Do you have any significant fears, phobias, or hang-ups? Identify five specific examples.**

....

....

....

3. **Are you prejudiced about anything? Give three examples.**

....

....

....

4. What qualities are you drawn to in other people (friends, significant others, etc.)?

....

....

....

5. How do you feel about yourself physically, intellectually, and socially?

....

....

....

6. What do you want most in your life?

....

....

....

SPY FOR A WEEK

It's easy to analyze people you know well. But how about everyone else out there? Do you know how to interact with others in a way that you learn something about their fears and desires in a way that both of you can benefit from the interaction? On page 63 of *Life Strategies for Teens,* you'll find a "Top

Ten List from Dorm 66 at the University of Texas," which is a list of the ten most common characteristics shared by virtually everyone you'll ever meet.

Tear that list out—or copy it down—and carry it around for a week. Take it out when you have some down time between classes, or when you're waiting for the bus, or for your friends after school. Use this list to spy on other people's behavior throughout the week. When you witness someone exhibiting one of the characteristics listed, put his or her initials beside that characteristic and briefly record the situation. For example, you see a classmate named Barbara snap at a guy for tripping over her backpack. The guy is embarrassed in front of everyone. This is unusual behavior for Barbara because she is the sweetest, least confrontational person around. If fact, she has trouble saying "no" to people because she doesn't want anyone to be upset with her. She's usually sensitive and kind, and people really like her because of that. Since this reaction is so not like Barbara, everyone, including the guy she yelled at, overlooks it because they realize that Barbara is just having a bad day. This incident is a perfect example of #9 on the list: Even good people have bad days. People are much more likely to understand and forgive someone for being snippy or rude if they know that they are normally kind, good, patient people.

I may have just given you a longer example than what you will need, but try paying attention to similar types of situations. In the course of your spying, find one example for each of the top ten characteristics and write down what happened. You'll begin to see that these characteristics, or impulses, are universal, and that people are likely to have them and respond to them in the same ways.

1. CHARACTERISTIC: ....

   What happened? ....

   ....

2. CHARACTERISTIC: ....

   What happened? ....

   ....

3. CHARACTERISTIC: ....

   What happened? ....

   ....

4. CHARACTERISTIC: ....

   What happened? ....

   ....

5. CHARACTERISTIC: ....

   What happened? ....

   ....

6. CHARACTERISTIC: ....

What happened? ....

....

7. CHARACTERISTIC: ....

What happened? ....

....

8. CHARACTERISTIC: ....

What happened? ....

....

9. CHARACTERISTIC: ....

What happened? ....

....

10. CHARACTERISTIC: ....

What happened? ....

....

Now that you better understand these ten characteristics of all people, including you and me, start thinking of how you can use them when you interact with others so that you can both get something you want.

DO SOMETHING DIFFERENT!

In the midst of all this self-discovery—which can be a bit tedious, let's admit it—have some fun by shaking up your routine a bit. I'm sure it's beginning to dawn on you that you can look at things from different perspectives and make different choices than those you have in the past. For the next week, try injecting a few new activities into your day-to-day. Exercise your power of choice. Do some things you've seen other people do and have wanted to do yourself. I have some suggestions here, but come up with some of your own, too.

★ Meet a friend for breakfast before school to chat and relax before the day begins. See how much more prepared and productive you feel than when you stumble into class barely awake as the first bell rings.

★ Go somewhere you haven't been–like a museum, a park, a new part of town, or a new movie theater–after school with some friends, or even by yourself. You'll feel much more engaged with the world than if you go straight home and turn on the TV or your PlayStation.

★ Go to a bookstore or library after school one day and choose a book to read just for fun (not because it was assigned).

★ Exercise in the morning *before* school, even if it's just for ten minutes.

★ Wear a "weird" shirt to school one day.

★ Get your homework done right away after school (instead of right before you go to bed) so you can have the evening free.

★ Ask your mom and dad to watch your favorite TV show with you.

What are five other new experiences you'd like to have, or small changes you'd like to make to freshen up your routine? List them in the space provided.

1. ....

2. ....

3. ....

4. ....

5. ....

LIFE LAW TWO
YOU CREATE YOUR OWN EXPERIENCE

Your Objective: Take responsibility for your life. Figure out what role you play in your own experiences—good and bad. Learn to make better choices so that you will be happier with the outcomes.

Life Law #2 is a little dose of tough love. When I say "You Create Your Own Experience," I mean that you are responsible for your whole life, your choices, your behavior, your responses to situations, your reactions to other people. Before we can ever realize the power that we have to control our own lives, we must realize that our choices, behaviors, and actions, and the results that come from them, have put us where we are today. I don't want you to think that every circumstance you've ever faced in life is your fault or within your control, of course not. But it is true that you have control over how you deal with every situation you encounter. Life Law #2 is all about taking responsibility for your life—including making changes to improve it. You create your own experience, so you might as well make it the best experience you can possibly imagine . . . starting now.

OWNING UP TO MY FEELINGS

The question you'll no doubt be asking yourself throughout your study of the Ten Life Laws is, "What do I want to be better in my life?" Perhaps it would be easier to start with the question, "What don't I like about my life?" Life Law #2 says that you are the one whose responsibility it is to change those things you don't like because the things that you don't like are, for the most part, responses to things that you are doing. If you change what you are doing, so too will you change the things in your life that you don't like. The first step you need to take is to put your finger on the ten things about your life that you are really not happy with and write them down in the following list. (You began to think about these things in the "What's *Really Not Working*" section in Part I of this workbook, so look back as necessary.)

1. ....

2. ....

3. ....

4. ....

5. ....

6. ....

7. ....

8. ....

9. ....

10. ....

It's not enough just to know what doesn't work in your life, you have to admit to how these less-than-ideal circumstances are making you *feel*. Are you sad, angry, lonely, resentful, hurt? Indicate how you feel under each circumstance. Now circle the three circumstances that you feel most urgent about improving. You're work is now cut out for you, you know where to begin. Focus only on these three things and figure out how you can work to make your life better. When you have improved those three aspects, move on to the other seven.

Below, write the life circumstance that you made number one in the preceding list.

LIFE CIRCUMSTANCE: ....

....

Now answer the following questions.

In the last year, what have I done to create, or Keep up, this circumstance (include decisions, reactions to others, etc.)?

....

....

What are three specific choices I made this year that have made me get caught up in this circumstance?

....

....

What are three specific opportunities I passed up to get myself out of this circumstance?

....

....

What advice have I ignored that would have helped me deal with this problem?

....

....

Is there anyone who can help me address this problem?

....

....

What specific *first action* must I take to begin my climb out of this circumstance? Is it talking to someone? Saying "no" this weekend when my friend offers me the opportunity to do something I know I shouldn't be doing? Is it going to the gym

tomorrow afternoon? Is it making an apology today?

....

....

STOP SAYING THAT ABOUT YOURSELF!

You have control over the negative conversations you hold with and about yourself every day. These bad things you say to yourself play over and over in your head like an ongoing tape player and they can completely control behaviors and choices if you let them. In fact, they keep you from doing the very things that will help you most because they keep reinforcing the idea that you can't change your behavior, that you can't make things better, that you're stuck. Here is a list of twelve negative tapes that I'm sure you've played to yourself before:

★ I'm not smart enough.

★ These other people are much more interesting (attractive, talented, etc.) than I am.

★ I'm not as good as the rest of these people.

★ I cannot and will not succeed.

★ I always quit.

★ No matter what I do, it won't make a difference.

★ They've already got their minds made up and I can't change them.

★ I'm just going through the motions; nothing ever changes.

★ They'll figure out how dumb I am.

★ I'm a girl, and they won't listen to a girl (okay, if you're a guy, you probably haven't said this).

★ I'm too young to do this.

★ I'm too old to do this.

Use these statements to help you figure out the negative tapes that you are playing to yourself. Now make a list of the top ten comments you use to assassinate your own character.

1. ....

2. ....

3. ....

4. ....

5. ....

6. ....

7. ....

8. ....

9. ....

10. ....

For the next week, pay attention to the nasty thoughts running through your head, those comments you make against yourself. Every time you say one of these things, make a note of it—on paper. Look at the grand total at the end of the week. The more aware you are of the poisonous ideas you're sticking yourself with, the better able you will be to get rid of them when they come along again.

"IF YOU LOOK AND ACT LIKE A DUMB-ASS . . ."

And now, here's a piece of good news: You choose the role you want to play in life (whether or not you believe it right now). And in doing so, you decide what kind of response you get from the world. You decide because you choose the behaviors that put you in each of these roles. Answer each of the following questions with one or two words, sometimes just "yes" or "no." Put a checkmark in the blank to the right of each question if you agree that *you choose to behave as you do in each instance.* If you do not believe that you choose the role you play in some cases, explain why that is.

1. How do you dress? _____

2. How do you talk? _____

3. What kind of friends do you have? _____

4. Who do you date? _____

5. Where do you hang out? _____

6. Do you respect those older than you? _____

7. What kind of friend are you? _____

8. Are you a hard worker? _____

9. Are you honest? _____

10. Are you a giver or a taker? _____

THE ROLES WE PLAY

So, what *is* the role you choose to play in the world? We all have an image of ourselves, whether it's the class clown or the homecoming queen. What image do you choose to play off to others? Here are some questions to help you figure that out. As always, be honest in your answers.

1. Stand in front of a mirror and study your clothes, your hair, and your posture. What do you think your appearance—your "look"—is saying to others? Is it the look that you want to project to others? Why have you chosen this look? Do you like the results, the responses that this look gets you?

....

....

2. Think about the way you meet strangers. How do you speak to them? What do you think is their first impression of you? Describe yourself through their eyes in the following space. Do they meet the real/best you? Do you look them in the eye? Do you speak clearly? What should you keep the same? What should you change?

....

....

3. How do you talk to your parents? Do you try to rebel by fighting, remaining silent, being sarcastic, etc.? Or, are you willing to listen and consider their side of the story? Is what you are doing getting the results you want? How would you respond if they

treated you in such a way? Is this the way you treat your friends? Do your friends treat you differently as a result?

....

....

4. What is your personality like around other students? Are you a giver or a taker? Are you warm or distant? What is their response to you? Do you like their response? How can you improve?

....

....

WHAT'S MY STYLE?

Whether you want to accept it or not, you play a big part in the way other people respond to and treat you. It all has to do with your behavior, particularly the way you present yourself to the world through your appearance, attitude, actions, and the way you treat others. We all have our own style—whether it's the way we talk, walk, or dress—that influences who we are and what others make of us. Read about some common styles on pages 72 through 77 of *Life Strategies for Teens;* I've listed them again here.

Before you can understand how the world responds to you (and how you can change that) based on your own style, begin by thinking about *your* response to other people based on their style. You must know at least one person who fits the description of each style in the following list. Write their name beside the style and then write about one instance in which you saw this person behaving in his or her typical fashion and the way people treated him or her in response.

_____ GOODY-TWO-SHOES: ....

EVENT: ....

Treatment received: ....

_____ PROM QUEEN: ....

EVENT: ....

Treatment received: ....

_____ TEASE: ....

EVENT: ....

Treatment received: ....

_____ JOCK: ....

EVENT: ....

Treatment received: ....

_____ THE WHINER: ....

EVENT: ....

Treatment received: ....

_____ DRAMA MAMA: ....

EVENT: ....

Treatment received: ....

_____ TEACHER'S PET: ....

EVENT: ....

Treatment received: ....

_____ GOSSIP: ....

EVENT: ....

Treatment received: ....

_____ SLACKER: ....

EVENT: ....

Treatment received: ....

_____ PERFECTO: ....

EVENT: ....

Treatment received: ....

_____ DRUGGIES: ....

EVENT: ....

Treatment received: ....

_____ GRANOLA: ....

EVENT: ....

Treatment received: ....

_____ THE GLAMOUR-PUSS: ....

EVENT: ....

Treatment received: ....

_____ BRAINIACS: ....

EVENT: ....

Treatment received: ....

_____ GREASERS: ....

EVENT: ....

Treatment received: ....

_____ PIG PENS: ....

EVENT: ....

Treatment received: ....

_____ MINIONS: ....

EVENT: ....

Treatment received: ....

_____ MARILYN MANSONS: ....

EVENT: ....

Treatment received: ....

Now go back and mark every style that describes you. In the following space, describe what you think your overall style is. Can you think of a name for it? Knowing your own style is important because it can help you figure out why people respond to you the way they do, and thus help you find a way to change the responses that you don't like.

....

....

....

....

Can you think of five instances in which someone responded to you in ways you did not want—were they angry, rude, cold, withdrawn, mean? What do you think it was about your behavior that caused this response?

1. ....

2. ....

3. ....

4. ....

5. ....

Of course, you're full of positive personality traits, too. What are the top five most positive things about you? Don't be modest—write them down! How do people usually respond to each of these qualities?

1. ....

2. ....

3. ....

4. ....

5. ....

LIFE LAW THREE
PEOPLE DO WHAT WORKS

Your Objective: Understand what "payoffs" are and learn what role they play in your behavior and the behavior of others. If you can control these payoffs, you will learn how to control your life.

Think about it: If something you do produces negative results for you, you're not going to do it again. So, if you are repeatedly doing something, it is most likely that on some level it is giving you a positive result or "payoff," even if the result is not something you enjoy. A good example of this is someone who always acts out in grade school because he or she wants attention, even if that attention is people screaming at and scolding him or her.

To break your bad behavior habits, you must first figure out what you're getting out of them and then rid yourself of that need or desire. Payoffs can be pretty subtle and, therefore, hard to detect. Of course, they can also be in-your-face obvious. The payoff for trading gossip, for example, could be knowing that with your valuable information comes a sense of power, an "in" to whatever group you're trying to get into. If you know what's going on, perhaps people will consider you to be one of the gang, and with the right kind of info, a very important member.

The following exercises are designed to help you determine what causes you to do certain things no matter what problems they cause you. I suggest you reread the examples I have provided on pages 89 through 91 in *Life Strategies for Teens* before you begin.

UNFULFILLED PROMISES

How often have you started a new school year or a new season or a new relationship by promising yourself that you'll do better, work harder, be more committed or interested this time? Check off any of the following statements that describe you. Then, in the space provided, list five of the most frustrating and persistent patterns in your life that you don't like, or wish you would quit. Write down anything you do, or any way you act, that makes you later say, "I wish I hadn't been that way."

- ☐ I eat when I'm not hungry.
- ☐ I lose my temper and argue with my parents and siblings.
- ☐ I give in to the demands of others when I know I shouldn't.
- ☐ I choke under pressure when I'm aiming for my best performance.
- ☐ I feel guilty even when I know I shouldn't, and so I respond by making decisions that are bad for me
- ☐ I spend a lot of time taking part in activities I don't really want to do.
- ☐ I spend my free time in front of the television when I should be exercising, spending time with my family or friends, or bettering myself somehow.
- ☐ I often procrastinate and do not get around to the projects that would make me feel better about myself.
- ☐ I talk about people behind their backs and often don't keep secrets when I'm supposed to.
- ☐ I agree to participate in an activity, but I get cold feet at the last minute and cancel or don't show up.
- ☐ I spend more money than I have. Buying things for myself makes me feel good at the time.

List the five repetitive behaviors that you most want to change.

1. ....

2. ....

3. ....

4. ....

5. ....

So, now you've figured out some of the things you do because you get an immediate reward or payoff. Unfortunately, while these activities make you think you're getting what you want, in the short-term they will only keep you from getting where you really want to go. Now it's time to start figuring out what the payoffs are for you.

You might consciously say to yourself that you don't like your behavior. You may not like the idea of your drinking at parties, or the idea of being sexually promiscuous. You may not like the idea of being withdrawn or rude around teachers and parents. You may not like the image of yourself as irresponsible, or lazy, or even dangerous. But at a subconscious level, these behaviors are giving you something that you want very much. They're giving you some sort of quick fix—a payoff. People don't repeat behaviors or behavior patterns unless they get something out of those behaviors at some level. You are not an exception, because *there are no exceptions!!* Look at the following list from

Life Strategies for Teens of common negative behaviors and payoffs. Add five more of your own negative behaviors (mild or extreme) and think hard about what the basic payoff is for each one. Write them down in the blank spaces that follow.

NEGATIVE BEHAVIOR	PAYOFF
Shyness	No risk of rejection if you reach out
Temper	Releasing tension, anger, or stress
Sarcasm	Don't have to show true emotions
Mediocrity	No pressure to perform
Showing off	Getting attention from others
Laziness	Don't have to get involved in life
....	....
....	....
....	....
....	....
....	....

WHAT'S GOT TO GO?

Let's get to the bottom of these bad behaviors by adding some details. In the spaces provided following the next paragraph, try to figure out the five most persistent, or hard-core, of your negative behaviors. Answer each of the following questions for each one of those nasty habits or attitudes:

IDENTIFY THE SPECIFIC BEHAVIOR.

1. When does this negative behavior happen?

....

2. How bad is this problem?

....

3. Why is this behavior bad, and what kind of damage is it doing to you?

....

4. What is the payoff?

....

EXAMPLE
BEHAVIOR: SMOKING POT

1. Every time I hang out with a certain group of people at certain parties, I join in whatever they're doing because I don't want to feel embarrassed for being outside the group or teased about being so straight.

2. This behavior is obviously very unhealthy for me because I am hurting my body by getting high.

3. I am also risking getting in serious trouble with the law, my parents, and my school and I'm not really happy or having fun doing these things.

4. My payoff is that I feel included, like part of the group, accepted.

Pretend you are a therapist speaking to a patient, or whatever it takes to get you to analyze yourself carefully. The harder you think and the more honest you are, the better this exercise will serve you. Now, begin:

BEHAVIOR #1:

1. ....

2. ....

3. ....

4. ....

BEHAVIOR #2:

1. ....

2. ....

3. ....

4. ....

BEHAVIOR #3:

1. ....

2. ....

3. ....

4. ....

BEHAVIOR #4:

1. ....

2. ....

3. ....

4. ....

BEHAVIOR #5:

1. ....

2. ....

3. ....

4. ....

Now, ask yourself the following about each of the five negative behaviors you've identified:

1. What does this behavior give me that I seem to want so much?

2. Does this behavior make me feel accepted, more in control, or grown up? If so, how? Does it actually give me more control, make me more mature, or am I just tricking myself?

3. What risks am I taking with this behavior? Are they worth it?

4. What risks am I avoiding with this behavior?

5. What pain or situation am I avoiding by acting this way? Am I actually avoiding the pain? Is this the best way to deal with it? Am I improving my situation or just avoiding it?

6. Am I trading short-term happiness or fun for longer-term satisfaction or fulfillment? If so, how?

7. Is it important for other people to see me acting this way? If so, what is my payoff for that? Am I proud of my behavior?

8. Do I behave this way because I believe it's what other people have come to want and expect from me?

9. Does this behavior really make my life easier? In what way?

10. Does this behavior make by life better?

11. How have these behaviors made my life worse?

CASH IN NEGATIVE PAYOFFS FOR POSITIVE PAYOFFS

Now, take your five negative behaviors from the previous section and analyze them in the following way. For each behavior or situation, think of cashing in the negative behavior for positive behavior so that you can reap the benefits that go along with it. What needs to change in order for that to happen?

1. Behavior that has got to go: ....

   The behavior that I want and will be most proud of: ....

   Potential positive payoff(s) of new behavior: ....

2. Behavior that has got to go: ....

   The behavior that I want and will be most proud of: ....

   Potential positive payoff(s) of new behavior: ....

3. Behavior that has got to go: ....

   The behavior that I want and will be most proud of: ....

   Potential positive payoff(s) of new behavior: ....

4. Behavior that has got to go: ....

   The behavior that I want and will be most proud of: ....

   Potential positive payoff(s) of new behavior: ....

5. Behavior that has got to go: ....

   The behavior that I want and will be most proud of: ....

   Potential positive payoff(s) of new behavior: ....

DO I FEAR RISK?

Being afraid of risks is part of being human. How many people would easily say, "Sure, I'll sky dive," or "Yeah, I'll tell everyone around me what I'm really feeling"? If you think about it, the two are not so different—sometimes you need to open yourself up to hurt in order to do something great. Taking risks of any kind means getting over your fears, your laziness, your lack of confidence; it means giving up the control we think we have and letting the chips fall where they may. It's easier just to stay where we are and not try to change a thing. But you've got to resist that temptation with all your might. Don't let yourself become addicted to what's familiar to you—doing the same thing all the time is about as boring and uncool as one can get.

Now, think about one of the five behaviors we've been dealing with that troubles you the most and picture your life without it. What would it be like to really follow through with making the changes you described? What risks will you be taking to get there? Are the risks worth taking? Are the risks really that risky and scary after all? Is this negative behavior really worth hanging on to? What will you be losing by giving up this behavior? Anything? What will you gain? Sure, failing may not be any fun, but being unhappy with your behavior is not much fun either. Remember, until you do something different, you will never receive different results.

Write a paragraph in the following space answering those questions and describing your new life without the bad behaviors. Write the script to your life the way you want it to be. Tell the story of your life having taken the risk to change what you are not happy with.

....

....

....

....

LIFE LAW FOUR
YOU CANNOT CHANGE WHAT YOU DO NOT ACKNOWLEDGE

Your Objective: Identify and admit to the problems in your life and start taking action to solve them instead of just sitting around, making excuses.

Let's face it, if you're not willing to acknowledge your problems and hang-ups, you'll never be able to change them. If you're not honest about how you're doing in life, and honest with yourself about what is and isn't working, then you're only causing more problems for yourself. If you don't know *where you are* in life, it will be impossible to get to *where you want to be*. Denial is less painful than honesty in the short run, but in the end, those of us with our heads stuck in the sand are going to pay—in bad relationships with ourselves and others. So, get real with yourself *now* and look your problems straight in the eye. Admit to the lies you've been telling yourself about yourself and your relationships. You'll be taking a huge weight off your shoulders when you do.

Think of this as going to the doctor. The first thing a doctor does is diagnose what is wrong because it's a huge waste of time to treat a head cold if you've just limped in with a sprained ankle. Diagnose the problems in your life so that you can spend your time making those situations better.

THE WEBS WE WEAVE...

Here's an exercise to help you figure out how often you manipulate the truth, either by telling white lies, leaving out certain pieces of information, or allowing someone to go on believing what isn't technically true. We all bend the truth here and there for a number of reasons: to avoid confrontation, to resist someone else's prying, to maintain our privacy, to present ourselves to the world in the best possible light. You need to know when you're doing this, and more important, why. If telling lies has become a habit, you know that's something you have to work on. Dishonesty, in all its forms, causes us to avoid or postpone facing the truth. When you think about it, dishonesty is a form of laziness—it's there to get us out of doing or saying something we don't want to do or say. The more honest you are with yourself, the more honest you'll be with the world around you.

Keep track of the fibs and white lies you hear yourself telling at school and at home this week. (Include omissions of truth and implying that something is true when it isn't.) Every time you hear a lie pass your lips, make a note of it by attaching a rubber band or safety pin to your backpack. How many do you have at the end of the week? Are you surprised at the number? Are you horrified or pleased? Now, make a conscious effort to decrease the amount of fibbing for the following seven days. Can you decrease the amount by half if you keep it at the forefront of your mind? When we allow ourselves to tell white lies to others, we also think it is okay to tell white lies to ourselves—and that prevents us from ever improving our lives.

REWRITE HISTORY A LITTLE

Think back over the past year or two to what you consider to be the biggest, most damaging lie you told during that time. In the following space, write a paragraph exploring what would have happened if you had decided to be truthful in that situation. How would the whole scenario have changed? How would the person (or people) to whom you told the lie have reacted? Would telling the truth have made your life more difficult? If so, would the effects have been short- or long-term? What would your payoff have been for telling the truth? Why were you initially afraid of the truth?

'FESSING UP

Think of ten things that you have trouble owning up to about yourself. What do you hate to admit to yourself? What about you makes you cringe and immediately try to get the story, lie, or action out of your head? After you identify that thing, explain *why* you have so much trouble admitting to this part of your personality.

EXAMPLE

I HATE ADMITTING TO MYSELF THAT I'M WILLING TO TRADE GOSSIP AND RUMORS IN ORDER TO BE POPULAR. THE REASON I HATE TO ADMIT THIS IS THAT I DON'T WANT TO BELIEVE THAT I'M A SHALLOW, DISLOYAL PERSON.

1. ....

2. ....

3. ....

4. ....

5. ....

6. ....

7. ....

8. ....

9. ....

10. ....

"IF YOU DON'T STAND FOR SOMETHING, YOU WILL FALL FOR ANYTHING"

One of the most common things we hate to admit to ourselves is the fact that we stop thinking for ourselves and allow other people, or the group, to decide where we're going and what we're doing. I'm talking specifically about *peer pressure*. Normal, smart, good people have been know to do the most mindlessly stupid and self-destructive things when they let other people make decisions for them—all because of the need to feel accepted.

Ask yourself what things in your life you have done because you felt pressure from your friends. Here's a list to start you thinking. Put a check mark next to any of the activities that sound familiar to you. In the blank spaces provided, write down ten more things you have done against your own best judgment because of peer pressure.

_____ Being defiant and disrespectful to your parents because your friends are to theirs

_____ Acting disinterested in school because only the "nerds" care about learning

_____ Drinking at parties because all the cool kids do

_____ Smoking marijuana or doing other drugs because it's the cool thing to do

_____ Having sex because it is expected and because you don't want to lose the relationship

_____ Sneaking out at night because "everybody else" is doing it

_____ Lying to your parents about where you are going because "everyone" is going to be there and you don't want to be left out

_____ Being rude or unkind to someone deemed "unacceptable" by the people you would like to be accepted by

_____ Giving up an interest or activity because others considered it uncool

_____ Behaving in a cruder, meaner, or more outrageous way than you would normally behave because people you want to impress are watching

_____ Holding back your own opinion about a topic because it wasn't the popular opinion

Now make your own list:

1. ....

2. ....

3. ....

4. ....

5. ....

6. ....

7. ....

8. ....

9. ....

10. ....

KNOW WHAT TO SAY NEXT TIME

If you at least acknowledge to yourself that you are being pressured, then you have a huge advantage. You can anticipate the pressure and prepare yourself to deal with it. You can decide ahead of time what to say to fight off the peer pressure. Take pride in the fact that you're not going to let anyone else run your life. Take pride in the fact that you know who you are and that you hold fast to your values.

Take a minute to list five behaviors that you know you don't want to take part in, but feel your "friends" wouldn't think you were cool if you didn't.

1. ....

2. ....

3. ....

4. ....

5. ....

Now list five comments you should be ready to say the next time you feel pressure. Pretend you're talking to someone who's really twisting your arm.

1. I'm not going to do that because: ....

2. I'm not going to do that because: ....

3. I'm not going to do that because: ....

4. I'm not going to do that because: ....

5. I'm not going to do that because: ....

Congratulations. You just took one more step out of denial and have pre-pared yourself to deal with peer pressure when just saying "no" doesn't work.

AM I STUCK IN MY COMFORT ZONE?

We live in denial when we don't admit to ourselves that we are not living up to our potential and doing the things that really mean something to us. Denial can be like a not very good old friend, someone that you don't really like, but hang out with just because that is what you've always done. They aren't great, but they're okay. We frequently do the same thing in our lives. You get to a place where you're comfortable but not very productive; every-thing is familiar but nothing is a challenge; you're doing "fine" but you don't have any real sense of satisfaction; you're in a routine but you never step outside of it to take any risks or try anything new. This is a comfort zone. Stepping out of our comfort zones is a bit like stepping out of a hot shower into the cold air. However, if you're really going to make progress, to expand your horizons, develop self-confidence, form new relationships, and take pride in your accomplishments, you've got to break out of this zone. Think of it this way: Your comfort zone is like a velvet coffin. It's warm, soft, and sheltering—but it's a coffin!

Here are a few guidelines that you can use to determine whether or not you are stuck in a comfort zone. Put a check next to any of the following statements if they apply to you. In the space that follows, list any more examples you can think of that show how you are trapped in a comfort zone.

_____ You're always bored.

_____ You don't ever challenge yourself.

_____ You feel that your accomplishments are pretty worthless.

_____ You think your daily after-school activities are mostly pointless.

_____ You don't seem to enjoy things the way everybody else does.

_____ You never keep your promises.

_____ You have no goals.

_____ You're a little scared of trying something new.

_____ You think your life doesn't have much of a purpose.

_____ You frequently say, "Nah, I'll just stay here and watch TV."

_____ You never challenge yourself.

____ You're not really interested in anything.

____ You always need to be entertained (by TV, movies, etc.) in a passive, nonparticipatory way.

____ You're not sure what you're good at because you haven't ever made an effort to develop any skills or talents.

____ You resist trying new, unfamiliar activities.

....

....

....

....

Sure, most of these problems won't destroy your life in one day, but if you don't pay attention, you end up spending every day at home doing nothing. Break out of the comfort zone and take some risks.

As you continue to come to terms with what you need to change in order to make your life happier and more successful, think again about the unhappy events in your life that have changed you dramatically. Choose what you consider to be the five most influential events. Maybe one of them is a lost love, or the death of a loved one. Maybe you had a falling out with a close friend. Maybe you've been violated in some way. Maybe you mistreated someone. Write down the five events in the following list.

The negative feelings that you have as a result of these events is like emotional baggage, and chances are, you're carrying some baggage with you from these events—you are feeling emotions like pain, guilt, anger, bitterness, mistrust, self-doubt, etc. These feeling may have, in turn, shaped parts of your personality in ways you would like to change. The first step toward replacing these negative feelings with new, more healthy feelings is acknowledging how you feel. Underneath each of the five life-changing events you have listed, write how you *feel* now about what happened. Perhaps you do not still feel strongly about the event and have moved on emotionally, or perhaps you need to work on the negative feelings that linger still.

EVENT: ....

Current emotional status: ....

EVENT: ....

Current emotional status: ....

EVENT: ....

Current emotional status: ....

EVENT: ....

Current emotional status: ....

EVENT: ....

Current emotional status: ....

Fortunately, the negative events you just described are only part of the story. There are times when we feel like everything is perfect, we forget about all of our problems and just have fun. Now do a little daydreaming. Describe such a time period, giving all the important details. Answer these questions somewhere along the way: What made you so happy? Did you realize how happy you were at the time, or only in retrospect? Why did you feel so good about yourself? Who were the important people in your life at the time? Where were you? What emotions did you feel? How did you feel when nobody else was around? What kind of future did you envision for yourself at the time? List all of the good feelings you were having about yourself (e.g. pride, confidence).

....

....

....

....

Now, what caused, or usually causes, this happy, best-time-you-can-remember to change? Why did it change? Did you change? Did something in your home life or school life change? Did a friendship end? Did you move? Write down as many details as you can remember.

....

....

....

....

Finally, how might you re-create some of the same conditions in your life now? What can you do to make now as fun as that time was? Think of the five things that made you happiest and write down each one in the following space. Below each thing that made you happy, write a suggestion for recapturing that same happiness now, something that you control and can do today!

EXAMPLE

I LOVED TO DANCE AND WORKED HARD TO BE THE BEST I POSSIBLY COULD BE. THEN, I HURT MY LEG AND I AM NOW UNABLE TO DANCE AS COMPETITIVELY AS BEFORE.

What I can and will do today to better my situation: I will find some hobby that I can work to perfect. I will challenge myself and do something I enjoy. For example: I will teach dance lessons or will work hard to rehab my leg—that is my new challenge.

1. ....

2. ....

3. ....

4. ....

5. ....

Don't forget that you are responsible for creating your own experience! If you do not like something in your life, find some way to better that situation. Remember, nobody will ever do it for you!

LIFE LAW FIVE
LIFE REWARDS ACTION

Your Objective: Make well thought out decisions and then take action and follow through. Understand that people are more interested in what you've done than what you plan to do.

It's one thing to say you're going to do something, or to think about it, or even to come up with a great strategy or idea for your pet project. It's something else to actually *do* it. Generally, people aren't as interested in your intentions, ideas, plans, or thoughts as they are in your action. You have to deliver the goods and that means taking action. In the end, you are the person who is going to be the most impressed and affected by the results of your action. It's so easy to make up excuses for postponing or canceling your plans to do or change something in your life—in the same way that it's easier to watch TV all week and then cram for your test the night before. The road to hell is paved with good intentions. The only thing that anybody ever cares about is results. Are you creating the results that you want in your life? In this next section, we are going to discuss how to take action in your own life to get more of what you want **today,** as well as prepare you to be more successful later in life.

GO HAVE SOME FUN

Do you ever catch yourself doing something not because it's fun and exciting, but because it's what you were doing yesterday? I know I do! Sometimes we don't even realize that we're in a rut, that our lives could use some excitement, challenge, and change. Routines are good—they provide us with important structure—but when routines become confining (no space for new activities, new friends, new skills, new behavior) they need to be changed.

Circle *admit* or *deny* in response to each of the following questions, based on how you really are living. Remember Life Law #4: Until you acknowledge a problem you will never be able to change it.

1. Do you spend all of your time outside of school watching the same old reruns and never leaving the couch?

   _____ Admit   _____ Deny

2. Are you addicted to a particular show or soap opera whose characters have become so real to you that you think about them, discuss them, and live through them even when you're not watching the show?

   _____ Admit   _____ Deny

3. Do you let your homework sit around undone until the last minute, and then rush through it, still watching TV?

   _____ Admit   _____ Deny

4. When your friends ask you to go out, do you always make an excuse to stay home?

_____ Admit   _____ Deny

5. Do you eat the same things all the time, even though you are sick of them?

_____ Admit   _____ Deny

6. Do you fantasize about doing things you never get around to doing (like forming a band with your friends)?

_____ Admit   _____ Deny

7. Is your personal upkeep headed south?

_____ Admit   _____ Deny

8. Is "no" your first response to most suggestions?

_____ Admit   _____ Deny

9. Has it been a long, long time since you met or spent time with someone new?

_____ Admit   _____ Deny

If you answered "admit" to four or more of these questions, you're in a rut, maybe even a serious rut. It's time you began to focus on how to get out of it.

"I HAD EVERY GOOD INTENTION . . ."

Life Law #5 states that life rewards action, **not intentions!** If you're any-thing like me, you've had every good intention of doing something that would improve your life (lose five pounds, try out for the team, audition for the play, volunteer at the hospital, visit a sick or lonely relative, teach your younger brother or sister how to do something, etc.), but instead you got talked out of it by laziness or you just flaked out and didn't make the effort. Think about the five big plans that you never followed through with in the past year. Write them down in the following list. Then write how you might have acted differently, instead of backing away from the plate. Next, write what positive results might have come from your taking action. Finally, write down one thing that you can still do to stop the pattern of not following through with the plans you make for yourself.

I intended to: ....

I should have: ....

The final result could have been: ....

I can still: ....

I intended to: ....

I should have: ....

The final result could have been: ....

I can still: ....

I intended to: ....

I should have: ....

The final result could have been: ....

I can still: ....

I intended to: ....

I should have: ....

The final result could have been: ....

I can still: ....

I intended to: ....

I should have: ....

The final result could have been: ....

I can still: ....

"I JUST CALLED TO SAY ..."

The older you get, the more you realize how important it is to tell people how much you care about them, how much you appreciate them, are grateful to them, and so on. Sadly, many of our best intentions that go unrealized have to do with the people we care about most. We think there will always be another opportunity to tell them how much we care, or tell them "thank you" or "I think you're great." But life is uncertain; we need to take the opportunity to tell people how we feel now. Make an appointment with yourself to tell those that you care about how you feel. This time, however, don't just "intend" to get it done, DO IT!! In the following space, list the five people to whom you would most like to give a special message. Write the message underneath the person's name. Then set a time to contact them (this week).

1. **NAME:** ....

   Message: ....

   I will contact them on: ....

2. **NAME:** ....

   Message: ....

   I will contact them on: ....

3. **NAME:** ....

   Message: ....

   I will contact them on: ....

4. NAME: ....

   Message: ....

   I will contact them on: ....

5. NAME: ....

   Message: ....

   I will contact them on: ....

BUT WAIT! THERE'S MORE!

The next part of your plan to put some excitement into your life is making sure that you don't fall back into your old, boring ways. Make three more commitments that you will act on this week. Remember, you have to *do* more to be and have more. Action is key.

In the following table I've identified four major categories of your daily life. Each one needs your attention and energy. Here's your chance to figure out where all of your time goes and how you can make it more worthwhile.

In each column, list the top four or five actions that you feel you need to take in that category. For example, the first row might read like this:

MY PERSONAL LIFE	MY SOCIAL LIFE	MY ACADEMIC LIFE	MY FAMILY LIFE
I need to take at least one day a week to call or go see my grandma.	I need to apologize to Jessica and Tonya so we can all be friends again.	I need to spend an extra fifteen minutes a day doing unassigned studying.	I need to find the time to have conversations with my parents every day so that we can know what is going on in each other's lives.

MY PERSONAL LIFE	MY SOCIAL LIFE	MY ACADEMIC LIFE	MY FAMILY LIFE
1._____	_____	_____	_____
2._____	_____	_____	_____
3._____	_____	_____	_____
4._____	_____	_____	_____
5._____	_____	_____	_____

TEN TIMES I'VE DROPPED THE BALL

Have you ever followed through on a plan, only to quit shortly thereafter? Why did you quit? It's important to get to the bottom of why you didn't follow all the way with your intentions. Quitting, dropping out, or dropping the ball never gives us any satisfaction at all. Every time we quit, we are telling ourselves and others that we are quitters. We begin to fear that we might not have what it takes to complete anything, to make good on our promises to ourselves. It's important to make following through a part of who you are now, because the older you get, the harder it will become to change this habit. List ten times you've failed to make good on an activity, relationship, commitment, or responsibility in the past several years. Beneath each one, explain why you dropped the ball. Did you get lazy, feel the work involved was too hard, lose interest . . . ?

1. ....

   Why? ....

2. ....

   Why? ....

3. ....

   Why? ....

4. ....

   Why? ....

5. ....

   Why? ....

6. ....

   Why? ....

7. ....

   Why? ....

8. ....

Why? ....

9. ....

Why? ....

10. ....

Why? ....

HERE'S WHAT I *HAVE* DONE

It is always good to try new things, and it's even good to try something else if you don't like what you just tried. But be sure that when you quit, it is not because you are scared, lazy, or stuck in a rut. Often, the experiences that require the most of you are also the most rewarding.

I know, I know: When are you going to have the chance to think about and list what you *have* done, what you did achieve, follow through with, make good on? Well, here's your opportunity. It is certainly important to keep in mind that your life story also contains plenty of things to be proud of, plenty of things to pat yourself on the back for. Thinking about your successes makes you determined to repeat them.

In the following space, list the fifteen best achievements in your life so far. What are you proud of? Being recognized as smart at school? The paintings you produced in art class? The large and adoring group of friends you have? Teaching your brother or sister how to do something? The great score you got on the SATs? Your encyclopedic knowledge of music trivia? Trying out for the team? The way you play the piano? Making varsity your freshman year? Having the highest average in trigonometry? Being the person everyone comes to when they can't solve a problem? Whatever it is, write it down here.

1. ....

2. ....

3. ....

4. ....

5. ....

6. ....

7. ....

8. ....

9. ....

10. ....

11. ....

12. ....

13. ....

14. ....

15. ....

How do you feel looking back over what you have achieved so far?

GET OUT THERE!

Resolve to take the risk, make the effort, and be persistent in the pursuit of your goals. Your life should be full of victories and rewards. If you are losing, that means someone else is winning. The winner might as well be you, but it's not going to happen by accident. It will happen because you make it happen. It will happen because you know what you want, and you move toward it in a strategic, determined, no-holds-barred manner.

Take out a piece of paper and make and sign a contract with yourself that, from now on, you will take action in your life to get more of the things you want. From now on, you will decide what you want, develop a strategy for getting there, and then take action immediately!

Sign this contract and carry it with you as a reminder that it is not okay to let opportunities pass you by.

LIFE LAW SIX
THERE IS NO REALITY, ONLY PERCEPTION

Your Objective: Figure out what lenses you are using to view the world around you and understand how that view can shape your reality for better or worse.

Each of us sees the world in our own way based on our personality, attitude, values, and point of view. So, without getting too philosophical about it, we can say that there is no one fixed reality. Instead, each of us creates our own reality out of a lifelong collection of perceptions. If your perceptions of your experience are consistently negative, unhappy, self-destructive, or distorted in some other way, your life is not likely to be very happy. You have to become aware of the "lenses" you put on when you go out into the world every day. How are they affecting, or warping, your image of the world?

THE LENSES WE USE

Reread pages 144 through 146 of *Life Strategies for Teens* to go over some common lenses through which most people view the world (the Me Lens, Peer Lens, "I'm in Love" Lens, etc.). These lenses are created and shaped by the experiences we have every day. For example, if one of the jocks at school is mean to you, you will often form a lens that tells you all jocks are mean. It is important to figure out what lenses you are looking through because seeing life with a warped perception can often make things seem worse than they really are. Now answer these questions:

1. What experiences in your life have caused you to wear lenses and what are those lenses?

2. Are these lenses good lenses? If so, in what way? (That is, do they allow you to view the world fairly and accurately? Do they protect you or do they hold you back?)

3. Do any of these lenses make your life more difficult than it needs to be? Do they prevent you from trusting other people, or make you depend on someone else for your happiness?

I HEAR VOICES

The way you *talk* is often a good predictor of how you see the world. Think back to the "tape recorder" exercise we did in Life Law #2 earlier in this workbook. The issue is not only how you talk to others, but also how you talk to yourself.

Search through your mind for reactions to the following three topics. Try to answer the questions with automatic, knee-jerk responses.

1. What are the things you automatically, reactively feel and believe about members of the opposite sex? (Examples: "Guys are macho and insecure." "Girls are two-faced.")

1. ....

2. ....

3. ....

4. ....

5. ....

2. What are the things you automatically, reactively feel and believe about teachers in general? (Example: "Teachers don't really care about me.")

1. ....

2. ....

3. ....

4. ....

5. ....

3. What are the things you automatically, reactively feel and believe about parents in general? (Example: "Parents don't listen.")

1. ....

2. ....

3. ....

4. ....

5. ....

What you just wrote are essentially your "tapes." These tapes are based on what we have experienced (or think we have experienced) in the past. But the question is: How true are these tapes for the here and now? Do you accurately evaluate each new situation or do you make a general assumption based on the tapes in your head?

MY TAPES ABOUT MYSELF

You need to be careful not only with the tapes you play about your friends, family, and teachers, but especially with the tapes that you play about yourself. Don't be fooled, there are NO positive tapes. You may be thinking, "But, Jay, isn't it good to tell myself that I am a good student and will do well on Monday's math test?" NO! Not unless you have prepared for this specific test and truly feel that on Monday, not just usually, you will do well. Don't fool yourself if you are not really prepared.

If all you're doing is thinking negative things about yourself, then you can bet your negative tapes are on a permanent loop inside your head. What if you are getting ready to compete in some way—sports, academic competition, audition—or to approach someone you have a crush on and every day, twenty-four hours a day, your head is filled with thoughts such as, "I'm not good enough," and "I know I can't do this," and "Nothing ever works out for me"? How do you expect to perform under the crushing weight of all this bad buzz about yourself?

The problem is not the reality of your life, it's what you're constantly telling yourself about your life. What are three negative tapes running through your mind today?

1. ....

2. ....

3. ....

For the next week, make a conscious effort to eliminate the tapes that are play-ing in your head. Every time one of these three tapes plays in your head, write it down on a card you carry with you. What is the final tally for the week? Have you made some progress since you first started examining your negative tapes in Life Law #2 of this workbook? The more aware you are of these tapes, the more you can control them. You have to realize that allowing taped messages to keep running in your brain will doom you to a life of just being okay when you can be great. The obstacles that you can build in your mind with this kind of talk take a long time and even harder work to overcome. Listening to those tapes often makes you your own worst enemy. But if you look at everything in the here and now, you open the doors to the possibility of success.

DID YOUR PERCEPTIONS FOOL YOU?

Back to filters and lenses and how you view the world.

First, you must admit how your point of view, which is often shaped by your tapes, affects your perception of reality. Begin by writing down, in the following list, ten specific instances in which you reacted negatively—for example, to a first meeting with someone; to a conversation that didn't go the way you wanted it to; to an encounter in a public place with a rude or thoughtless person; to a poor test score or evaluation; to the election of class officers or prom king and queen (where you felt the elections were unfair); and so forth.

To complete this exercise, you need to be willing to say to yourself, "The way I see things is just that, the way I see them." Someone you think acts like a snob might really just be shy. The rude and thoughtless person in line at McDonald's might have been reacting to something bad that just happened to him or her. Your enemy might have been named captain of the team not because he's the coach's favorite, but because the captain has the highest GPA and, though you didn't know it, the school now insists on this policy.

List ten instances in which you reacted negatively. Underneath each event, step outside of your own perceptions for a minute and look at the event from another angle. What might you have missed? What did you ignore? What weren't you aware of?

1. ....

Maybe this is really what happened: ....

2. ....

Maybe this is really what happened: ....

3. ....

Maybe this is really what happened: ....

4. ....

Maybe this is really what happened: ....

5. ....

Maybe this is really what happened: ....

6. ....

Maybe this is really what happened: ....

7. ....

Maybe this is really what happened: ....

8. ....

Maybe this is really what happened: ....

9. ....

Maybe this is really what happened: ....

10. ....

Maybe this is really what happened: ....

BELIEFS THAT HAVE BECOME BLINDERS

Persistent, pessimistic thoughts about yourself can do a lot of harm to your self-image. These unflattering, and often just downright mean, beliefs can literally become blinders that allow you to see yourself in only one way—negatively. They can only limit you because you approach every situation like a skittish, blinkered horse, thinking the same self-defeating thoughts about who you are. Free yourself from these damaging beliefs! In order to do that, you must first put your finger on what you are really telling yourself. Below is a list of comments I have heard many teens (including myself) make over the years. Do any of the same thoughts run through your head? Put a check mark beside each one that applies to you.

_____ I'm not very smart.

_____ I'm always the least talented in any competition.

_____ I wasn't made to win.

_____ No matter how good things look at first, something always gets in the way of my success.

_____ I cannot really change; I just am who I am.

_____ I don't have the family background to be what I really want to be.

_____ I've never been able to do it before; why get my hopes up now?

_____ If I get too happy and relaxed, something will go wrong.

_____ I worry that people are going to find out how much I don't know or can't do and they'll think I'm a fake.

_____ People wouldn't like me as much if I changed.

_____ I don't deserve a second chance.

Continue this list by writing ten more of your own beliefs that have become blinders in your life.

1. ....

2. ....

3. ....

4. ....

5. ....

6. ....

7. ....

8. ....

9. ....

10. ....

DEBATE YOURSELF AND LOSE

We all have deeply rooted attitudes or beliefs about ourselves and the world around us, especially about the people we come into contact with the most. It is important to make those perspectives more flexible, even to the point where you might have to toss them out all together and replace them with new ones. In the final exercise of this chapter, pretend you are debating . . . yourself.

Think about your closely held beliefs about the following people or things and then write them down. Then come up with other perspectives to counter your fixed beliefs. Turn things on their heads. Imagine how you *could* choose to see things.

YOUR RELATIONSHIPS WITH YOUR MOM AND DAD:

OLD BELIEFS: ....

....

NEW PERSPECTIVE: ....

....

ADULTS IN GENERAL:

OLD BELIEFS: ....

....

NEW PERSPECTIVE: ....

....

YOUR RELATIONSHIP WITH YOUR BROTHER(S) AND/OR SISTER(S):

OLD BELIEFS: ....

....

NEW PERSPECTIVE: ....

....

YOUR FRIENDS:

OLD BELIEFS: ....

....

NEW PERSPECTIVE: ....

....

YOUR RELATIONSHIP WITH YOUR BOYFRIEND OR GIRLFRIEND:

OLD BELIEFS: ....

....

NEW PERSPECTIVE: ....

....

YOUR ACADEMIC CAREER:

OLD BELIEFS: ....

....

NEW PERSPECTIVE: ....

....

YOUR FUTURE:

OLD BELIEFS: ....

....

NEW PERSPECTIVE: ....

....

YOUR TEACHERS:

OLD BELIEFS: ....

....

NEW PERSPECTIVE: ....

....

YOUR ENEMIES:

OLD BELIEFS: ....

....

NEW PERSPECTIVE: ....

....

You can't clean your room until you get rid of the trash, so throw out all those negative ideas and have fun starting over!

LIFE LAW SEVEN
LIFE IS MANAGED; IT IS NOT CURED

Your Objective: Learn that taking charge of your life is something you have to do every day.

The truth is that no matter how well you manage your life, you will still have to deal with problems that come up (and trust me, if there is one thing you can always count on, it is that life is full of problems). As long as you are prepared to deal with these challenges, you'll be okay. But life will be an easier ride if you first accept the fact that it is a series of obstacles—from mild to extreme—and know that, with the right skills in place, you will have won half the battle each time.

Think of yourself as the manager of a movie star. Think of what a manager is paid to do for that star: They make good decisions for the actor's career, image, relationships, and finances, and give them the best possible help in all other matters. As a manager of an important person, you are expected to do everything in your power to help him or her be successful, satisfied, happy, and healthy. Now make yourself that "important person," that "star." *You* are your own manager, and it is your responsibility to find and achieve the best things for each area of your life.

The exercises in this chapter are going to help you improve those managing skills, they will give you the knowledge you need to best control and direct your life.

HOW IS YOUR LIFE MANAGER DOING?

I hope I've got you thinking about yourself as a "life manager," as though you were a separate person hired to manage your life. Pretend that you are calling that other person, your highly paid manager, in for a life management evaluation. Remember that the one thing that counts in your evaluation is the *results* your life manager has produced for you, especially in the last year. Intentions don't count. What your life manager promised or hoped to do doesn't matter, the only thing that matters is what he or she has actually done. For each statement below, rate your life manager on a scale from 1 to 5 (1 = almost never, 3 = half of the time, 5 = almost always).

_____ My life manager is making well-thought-out, researched decisions.

_____ My life manager is making sure that I always put my best foot forward.

_____ My life manager is putting me in the right place at the right time.

_____ My life manager is taking care of my body.

_____ My life manager is taking care of my mind by stimulating and challenging it.

_____ My life manager is taking care of my emotions by not putting me in situations that will cause me problems.

_____ My life manager is choosing good relationships for me.

_____ My life manager is encouraging me to take some positive risks.

_____ My life manager is making sure that I have some time to unwind and reflect every day.

_____ My life manager is helping me meet new people and create new friendships.

_____ My life manager makes sure that I am having fun.

_____ My life manager shows me how to feel good about myself.

How is your life manager doing based on this quick evaluation? (The highest possible score is a 60 and the lowest is a 12.) Remember, your life manager is going to be with you forever, whether you like it or not, so begin to demand the results you want.

WHAT ARE YOU DOING WITH ALL THAT TIME?

It would be helpful to know how you, as your own life manager, are booking your time, day in and day out. Where are you directing most, too much, or not enough energy? Is your schedule so demanding that you don't have a moment to catch your breath and collect yourself? Does your life manager plan too little activity for you? Are you wasting precious time that you could be using to seriously go after an interest? Is your schedule imbalanced with too much play and not enough work, or vice versa? How would the best life manager in town schedule your life?

For the next week, keep a log of how you spend your time. I've divided all activities into four major categories to make it simple. Write down how much time you spent in each category during each day and describe what the specific physical, intellectual, social, and "other" activities were. Physical activities are just that: sports, dance, hiking, mountain biking, walks in the park, team practice—the focus is on working your body. Intellectual activities may be a school-related (academic teams, homework, time spent in class) or something you do independently for pleasure (reading a novel or the newspaper, going to a museum or performance, etc.). Social activities are just that: being social, making friends and hanging out with them, getting to know people a little better. Keep in mind that socializing can occur with people of all ages, not just friends your age. Use the "Other" column as a catch-all for anything else, from watching television to working at a job to running errands.

TIME LOG

	PHYSICAL	INTELLECTUAL	SOCIAL	OTHER
	What/How Long	What/How Long	What/How Long	What/How Long
SUN.				
MON.				
TUES.				
WED.				

THURS. ....

FRI. ....

SAT. ....

<u>TOTAL
TIME</u> ....

What does your schedule look like? What do your activities say about you? What interests you, what are your priorities? Do you feel that you need to make some adjustments so that you are paying more attention to certain categories and perhaps giving less time to certain activities? Do you feel unproductive after surveying what you have done for the week? Based on what you have observed about how you spend your time, what are five changes you need to make in the way you organize your schedule? Under each change, write how it would positively affect your life.

1. ....

2. ....

3. ....

4. ....

5. ....

YOUR LIFE IS NOW ON PROJECT STATUS

Now that you've realized what areas of your life need more (or less) attention, come up with five concrete plans to rearrange your time and energy. Examples: "Instead of spending two hours at the gym every day, I'll spend one hour at the gym and one hour at a coffee shop reading for fun," or "I'll stay home one night every weekend to hang out with my family or catch up on some studying, instead of going out and hanging with my friends like I always do," or "I'll go directly home after practice in the afternoons so I can get a headstart on my homework," or "I'll stop hanging out at the basketball courts with my teammates until dinnertime." List five adjustments that you should make in your life.

1. ....

2. ....

3. ....

4. ....

5. ....

After one week, have you been able to turn these plans into action? How does it feel? Are you more satisfied?

WHAT ARE PRIORITIES MADE OF?

Now that you have started moving in the right direction, what are some other life decisions; decisions that you make and then don't think about any longer, decisions that are not made daily but instead just once? What are the decisions that you can and need to make now that will improve the quality of your life and make you a better manager of it? These life decisions may very well be things that will force you to stretch and work a little more than you are used to. But in order to get more of what you want and less of what you don't want out of life, you have to be willing to do the work. What are your ideas for five important decisions that will have a real impact on your life and give it a clear, meaningful direction? Here are some examples to get you thinking; these major decisions have improved either my own life or my friends' lives in dramatic ways.

★ I will not drink and drive.

★ I will not mistreat or make fun of people who are considered "uncool".

★ I will not steal.

★ I will not blame others for my problems or faults.

★ I will not say hurtful, spiteful things to my parents.

★ I will not gossip.

★ I will not mistreat my body.

★ I will treat people with dignity and respect.

★ I will make decisions for myself about what I am willing to do and what I am not willing to do.

★ I will get out of unhealthy relationships with a friend or a boyfriend/girlfriend.

First, write down five life decisions that you have already made and know are part of your life.

1. ....

2. ....

3. ....

4. ....

5. ....

Now, list five life decisions that you would like to make part of your life. Understand that these are not casual commitments you are making. These are hardcore principles by which you plan to manage your life day in and day out.

1. ....

2. ....

3. ....

4. ....

5. ....

TURNING DREAMS INTO GOALS

The big difference between a dream and a goal is that dreams are kind of fuzzy and vague, and goals are very clear and specific. Choose one dream you have and then complete the following exercise with this single dream in mind.

1. *Translate your dream into specific events or behaviors that define what you want.* (It is not enough to say you want to be a good student. You have to define "good student" specifically and behaviorally. What does it mean in the real world?)

2. *Translate your dream into things that you can measure.* (For example, if you want to make the soccer team, what does that mean? What kind of training must you do? What are your strengths? Your weaknesses as a player? Translate your dream into what can really happen.)

3. *Assign a timeline to your goal.* ("Someday" is not a day of the week. You have to make a commitment to when you want what you want. By setting a timeline to your goal, you will hold yourself to a schedule rather than just hoping that it will happen "someday.")

4. *Choose a goal that you can control.* (A goal has to involve things to which you have access. There is no point in setting a goal to be taller so you can be a better basketball player. But what you can do is set a goal to "play big." You can build your leg

strength so that you can jump higher than somebody a foot taller than you. That's something you can control.)

5. *Plan a program and a strategy that will get you to your goal.* (What is the overall picture—the roadmap?)

6. *Define your goal in terms of steps.* (If you want to get better grades in the next six weeks, doing so will be the product of lots of small steps made each and every day. It won't be some giant leap you make all at once.)

7. *Create accountability toward the progress of your goal.* (Figure out some way to hold yourself accountable for what you say you are going to do. Maybe you can explain the commitment to a friend and have them check on you every day or every week. Or maybe you can require that you write down your progress every day. Either way, make sure that you have some way of holding yourself accountable on a regular basis.)

If you follow these seven steps, you will be setting yourself up for success and taking one more big step toward becoming a world-class life manager.

LIFE LAW EIGHT
WE TEACH PEOPLE HOW TO TREAT US

Your Objective: Learn that you have more control than you think you have over the way other people treat you. Learn how to *teach* people to treat you differently.

Relationships are, and always will be, an important part of our lives. You have a relationship, whether you want to or not, with everyone from your family members to your teachers, classmates, boss, coach, minister, doctor, neighbor, and so on. It would be a whole lot easier if, in all of these relationships, we were treated just as we'd like to be: with dignity, respect, trust, etc. Life isn't so easy, of course, so we have to learn how to make relationships as positive and healthy as possible. One of the most important lessons I've learned from growing up with my dad is that we all have more control than we feel we do over how other people interact with us. This is because we teach them how to treat us in the first place, through our own behavior, attitudes, and personality. The simple equation is this: If I show myself to be a respectful, mature, all-around good kid who gets decent grades and tries hard, my teachers are going to think highly of me and will treat me as someone worthy of responsibility, independence, and trust. Likewise, if I continuously prove to my parents that I break my word and am generally untrustworthy, they are more likely to severely limit my freedom. If you have established a relationship with someone, and you do not like and want to change that relationship, you are responsible for renegotiating it with them. The following exercises will show you how. But let's take a closer look at your current situation (if you haven't figured it out by now, making your life better means you have to look at it through a microscope).

YOU AND YOUR PARENTS

Your relationship with your parents is likely to be the central one in your life at the moment. Use the following questionnaire to focus on that relationship and to identify where there is room for improvement and renegotiation.

1. Are you clueless as to how to show your parents that you really respect them?

☐ YES　　☐ NO

2. Do you feel "too young" to get what you want?

☐ YES　　☐ NO

3. Do you feel as though your parents don't listen to you?

☐ YES　　☐ NO

4. Have you gotten into the habit of tuning your parents out and not hearing what they have to say?

☐ YES　　☐ NO

5. Do your parents give you long lectures including a list of "you should have" . . . ?

☐ YES　　☐ NO

6. Have you stopped bothering to let your parents in on your thinking, your ideas, hopes, plans—your life?

☐ YES   ☐ NO

7. Do your parents like to give you a history lesson about when they were teenagers?

☐ YES   ☐ NO

8. When you bring up a problem of yours, do your parents just try to top it with one of their own?

☐ YES   ☐ NO

9. Do you find that you only go to your parents when you have a problem?

☐ YES   ☐ NO

10. Do you feel that your parents treat you as if you were much younger than a teenager?

☐ YES   ☐ NO

11. When you're hanging out with your family at home, do you suddenly act more childishly than you would if your friends were around?

☐ YES   ☐ NO

12. Do you feel totally ignored?

☐ YES   ☐ NO

13. Do you feel put down and condescended to?

☐ YES   ☐ NO

14. Do you speak to your parents as if they don't have a clue in the world about anything that really matters in life?

☐ YES   ☐ NO

15. Do you feel hurt by the way your parents treat you?

☐ YES   ☐ NO

16. Do you think your parents feel hurt by the way you treat them?

☐ YES   ☐ NO

17. Are you kind to your brother(s)/sister(s)?

☐ YES   ☐ NO

18. Do you ever have the "whatever, it doesn't matter" attitude toward your responsibilities around the house?

☐ YES   ☐ NO

RENEGOTIATING WITH YOUR PARENTS

Even if our parents set boundaries and limits that we have to follow, we can still have some power over what those boundaries are. Sometimes, if we are smart, we can get them to widen the boundaries within which we operate—all because we teach them how to treat us. What are you going to do to change the way they treat you? All you have to do is teach them to treat you in a different way, in a way that you both enjoy.

Think about it: Every time you and your parents interact, you respond in some way. Your response totally influences whether the reaction you get from your parents will repeat itself in the future or not. If your parents tell you something you don't want to hear, and you blow up, yell, scream, stomp off to your room, and slam the door, then you have rewarded their strictness by making them think that you are even less mature than they expect you to be. Once again, you ended the interaction and let them off the hook. To change your relationship with your parents for the better, all you have to do is change some key actions and reactions that you throw out there. If you interact with your parents in any of the following ways, it will help you to gain more freedom and respect from them. Remember, you decide how your parents will treat you because frequently they are simply reacting to the way you are treating them. In the space provided beneath each suggestion, write down specific instances in which you have done the *opposite* of what is suggested.

1. Start a conversation with your parents.

....

....

2. Stay calm and don't take the bait.

....

....

3. Express interest in your parents' lives.

....

....

4. Stop demanding and start earning your freedom.

....

....

5. Inspire confidence and trust through your own accountability.

....

....

6. Allow yourself to be influenced by your parents' advice.

....

....

7. Be easy to get along with.

....

....

8. Talk to your parents at times other than when you have a problem or need

something.

....

....

Now, choose four of these eight suggestions and write them down on a note card that you will carry with you for the next two weeks. Make a notation beside each suggestion for every time you ignore the piece of advice and do the opposite. Use a different symbol to record the times you *do* interact with your parents in the way I suggest.

Keep in mind that if your parents are resistant at first, it is because you taught them to be that way. You got them into a routine of how to treat you and how to react to you—you have helped them to form a habit of mistrust and misunderstanding. Habits can be tough to change but it *is* possible. Keep trying; this will work! I promise you.

RENEGOTIATING WITH YOUR PEERS

Your power and ability to change relationships is not limited to the relationship you have with your parents. You may be just as frustrated with that jerk at school who keeps picking on you. You are sick of him hiding your backpack or cutting in front of you in line or just making you feel like a moron when everyone is looking. Or maybe you're fed up with the school gossip, who spreads nasty stories about you behind your back. Good news: As in the relationship with your parents, you have a huge amount of power and influence over this situation as well. You can change it today. You can change it because, once again, we teach people how to treat us; they don't decide on their own. Make the decision, right now, that you will not give up and accept treatment that you don't want. You do have control; you do teach people how to treat you. Remember, you are not a victim. Your job is to find out what "payoffs" (remember those?) you are creating that prompt others to treat you like they do.

Make a list of the five most difficult relationships in your life right now, excluding family members. In the first space underneath the person's name, describe what it is about this person that bothers you. In the second blank space, write what you think this person's payoff is for treating you this way. In the third blank, come up with a way to eliminate this payoff, a way to teach them differently.

EXAMPLE

NAME: **BILL** ....

1. Treatment: Cold and distant, he does not include me in the group unless he needs my help in math.

2. Payoff: I keep giving him my help whenever he wants it, no matter how he treats me later.

3. Eliminate payoff: Next time, I'll make it clear that I'm not at his beck and call. He will respect me more if I stand up for myself. He will know he can't take advantage of me, and will have to treat me with respect.

NAME: ....

1. Treatment: ....

....

2. Payoff: ....

....

3. Eliminate payoff: ....

....

NAME: ....

    1. Treatment: ....

    ....

    2. Payoff: ....

    ....

    3. Eliminate payoff: ....

    ....

NAME: ....

    1. Treatment: ....

    ....

    2. Payoff: ....

    ....

    3. Eliminate payoff: ....

    ....

NAME: ....

    1. Treatment: ....

    ....

    2. Payoff: ....

    ....

    3. Eliminate payoff: ....

    ....

NAME: ....

   1. Treatment: ....

....

   2. Payoff: ....

....

   3. Eliminate payoff: ....

....

MY SOCIAL WORLD

In addition to your family members, who are you closest to? It is important to sketch this out for yourself so that you can think about your relationships with all of these people as you complete the final exercise of this chapter. In the diagram below, put yourself in the center circle. In the outer circle, write the names of all of the people (no matter what age) you trust and feel closest to.

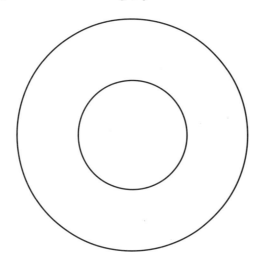

WHO, ME?

Now, let's put the shoe on the other foot. Just as it's true that you have allowed other people to treat you in ways you did not like, the people in your life have no doubt let you get away with not-so-Mr.-Nice-Guy behavior. Perhaps they've gone so far as to allow you to mistreat them without making it clear to you that your behavior was unacceptable. Or, maybe they've simply let you get away with behaviors that are unhealthy for you: drinking too much at a party, avoiding talking about a problem, lying. Could it be that you need to be turned around by some of the people in your life for the way you've behaved and treated them? Put a check mark beside any of the five following statements that describe you. Then record ten instances of bad or unhealthy behavior that your friends have let you get away with.

_____ I push others until they give in and I get my way.

_____ When I'm feeling defensive, I lash out at others and say unkind things that I later regret but don't apologize for.

_____ Instead of speaking directly to someone I'm having a problem with, I talk about him or her with another friend.

_____ I bail out of plans when something better comes along.

1. ....

2. ....

3. ....

4. ....

5. ....

6. ....

7. ....

8. ....

9. ....

10. ....

Is there something you can do (of course there is, and you know it!) to change these patterns? The more you give to your relationships and the more you hold yourself accountable for your treatment of other people, the happier you will be. Choose what you consider to be the five worst behavioral problems you have and take action today by addressing them. Can you make an apology? Reach out to someone who always reaches out to you? Have a serious discussion with someone about a problem in your relationship that you'd like to solve?

Think about how you feel toward those who have hurt you or treated you in a way that you didn't like, yet you have never said anything about it. This should motivate you to treat those you care about better, even though they have not yet complained. They will respect you and treat you better for doing so.

LIFE LAW NINE
THERE IS POWER IN FORGIVENESS

Your Objective: Learn that the anger and bitterness you're holding on to is doing more harm to you than anyone else. Understand how you may have given up control to the very same people who have wronged you; you must learn to reclaim that control.

Since life isn't perfect, we all get hurt and we are all given reasons, throughout life, to feel wronged and bitter and angry. The worst thing about this is that the resentment and hatred we carry around with us only makes the original hurt worse. It's like suffering double (or permanently) when you take on the negative emotions like a hundred-pound weight on your shoulders. Think about it: When you stay mad (which is no fun for you), you are just continuing to do what those who have wronged you started doing in the first place. Perhaps you don't realize it, but feeling angry, bitter, and blameful takes a lot of energy—energy we could be putting to good and productive use somewhere else.

Life Law #9 allows you to toss all that away, to free yourself from negative thoughts and emotions. It also states that forgiveness is a choice and, best of all, something you can decide to do rather than something you must wait for. When you are really, really angry with someone for hurting you, you are, in many ways, unable to get that person out of your mind. You've created a miserable bond with someone, as if you were handcuffed together. How liberating it would be to break that bond, to let the feelings go, and move on to something else!

Let me clarify—forgiveness is not so much about the other person and whether or not he or she deserves to be forgiven, as it is about you. *You* deserve to be free of bitterness and hurt. Not only that, those horrible, negative feelings you nurse inside will, like some alien virus on the *X-Files,* seep into your other relationships and keep them from being healthy. You don't want that!

TURNING FORGIVENESS INTO ACTION: "I'M OUT OF HERE" RESPONSE

Can you do it? Can you forgive? The "how to forgive" is not easy, but it can be done. The first thing you have to understand is that forgiveness is not a feeling; it is a decision. Fortunately, you don't always have to feel forgiving in order to forgive, to set yourself free from an emotional prison. You simply have to make the decision that you will not let the person who has hurt you affect your life for another day.

I want you to begin to understand and use the "I'm out of here" response, which is the very least that you have to do in order to get emotional closure with whomever has hurt you. This response is going to be different for every person in every situation. For example, if some waiter is rude to you in a restaurant and it really ticks you off, maybe your response is simply to leave and never return, knowing that you have made your statement that way. If the act made against you is much more serious, then much more is required. Maybe it involves talking to someone face-to-face, or writing a strong letter even if you never mail it. Maybe it even means telling someone that a relationship simply has to end because it no longer does you any good, that it's unhealthy, or that it causes you pain.

What you want to do is identify the *least demanding* thing you can do that will allow you to get emotional closure. Figure out who in your life has you locked in a state of bitterness and resentment, and then decide how to end it with that person and with your own negative feelings.

Let's go through that process right now. The following five steps, if followed, will allow you to achieve emotional closure and take your power back.

A. Search your mind and heart and identify all of those people who, in your opinion, have hurt you in a way that has filled you with negative emotions. Use the following five spaces to list these people one by one. If there are more, list them on the side of the page.

1. ....

2. ....

3. ....

4. ....

5. ....

B. Now, describe specifically what it is these people have done to you and, therefore, what you must forgive and learn to get over.

1. ....

2. ....

3. ....

4. ....

5. ....

C. Now, identify your "I'm out of here response" for each of these people. Do you need to confront them? Or, can you handle this entirely within yourself? Do you need to write them a letter? Do you need to call the police? What, with the least effort, will allow you to say, "This is it, it is all over, I am out of here"?

1. ....

2. ....

3. ....

4. ....

5. ....

D. Now, write the words you need to say to yourself to claim the freedom that comes from forgiveness.

1. ....

2. ....

3. ....

4. ....

5. ....

E. Lastly, take a moment to write down how you will feel once you are free of the negative emotions that have had you locked in a bond with this person. Be very specific!

1. ....

2. ....

3. ....

4. ....

5. ....

LET YOURSELF OFF THE HOOK

You're not doing yourself any favors or making anything better if you go through life feeling imprisoned by guilt, shame, or anger toward yourself. We all make mistakes and do and say things we later wish we had never done or said. Sometimes we do pretty bad things that haunt us for a long time afterward. But allowing this self-directed anger and torture to circulate in your bloodstream day after day is like poisoning yourself. How can you forge ahead with your life and make the necessary changes and improvements if you can't let go of your bad feelings about yourself? If you can forgive other people, you can forgive yourself. Remember, forgiveness is a decision, it doesn't always have to be just an emotion. Don't let yourself stop trying in life because you feel like you don't deserve to have fun. Forgive yourself and make your life better immediately! It is hard at times, but you must do it. Part of what will help you forgive yourself is making some kind of amends for what has caused you so much self-loathing. Obviously, those amends are going to be different for different situations; you won't treat breaking someone's heart as you would breaking someone's beeper. On the page below, describe the thing in your life you feel most guilty about or ashamed of.

What is it?

....

....

What have the after-the-fact feelings done to your behavior?

....

....

What have they done to your relationships (with yourself and others)?

....

....

What do you need to do in order to put the guilt to rest? What is your "I'm out of here" response to yourself?

....

....

WHAT ARE YOU PROUD OF?

Enough with the negativity already. At a certain point, you need to remind yourself of what you have going for you, what you have to feel proud of. As soon as you can lay the guilt and shame aside, you can take these good qualities in the right direction. Remind yourself of what you have to offer. Check off any of the following statements that describe you. Add your own at the bottom; there should be many.

_____ I am a loyal friend.

_____ I am a generous person.

_____ I care about other people and they know it by the way I behave.

_____ I have a great sense of humor.

_____ I put other peoples' needs before my own.

_____ I help other people feel good about themselves.

_____ People know they can trust and count on me.

_____ People come to me when they need support.

_____ I am a hard worker.

_____ I am patient and accepting.

_____ I am good to my family.

_____ I keep calm when things get tense.

_____ I am easy to get along with because I'm friendly and warm.

_____ I am interesting to talk to and have a good time talking to others.

....

....

....

....

....

....

....

....

The next time you start to get down on yourself, remember this list. And remember that life is too short to be mad and upset all the time. Forgive yourself and others and move on. Make the decision to put the bad behind you today and go have some fun!

LIFE LAW TEN
YOU HAVE TO NAME IT BEFORE YOU CAN CLAIM IT

Your Objective: Figure out what you want and then go get it.

What I'm about to say should come as no surprise: Before you can get what you want in life, you have to know what it is you want; otherwise, you'll just be running around in circles. You should be able to say clearly and specifically what it is that will make your life just how you want it. You should be able to say: "I want to get above a 3.8 GPA so that I can get into the University of Texas." "I want to date someone who treats me right, likes the same things I do, is mature, is nice to my family, and who makes me feel great about myself." "I want to make All-County in basketball." "I want to be cast in one of the two leading roles in the spring musical." "I want to stop fighting with my sister; I'd like for us to be close." "I want to go to the beach this summer with Mike, Ramsey, John, Jordan, and have a great time there."

In declaring to yourself what you want, you should be ambitious and realistic at the same time. Learn to distinguish between what *you* want and what other people want for you; between what will really make you happy and what you think looks good; between what you want to occur versus the feelings you want to have. Be specific but flexible, and take action to get what you want!

OUT, OUT!

Before you put in writing what you want your life to look like, think first of what you can throw out or get rid of. What *don't* you want? You've done enough self-examination throughout these chapters to make this part pretty easy. What behaviors, relationships, attitudes, and habits are weighing you down, getting you nowhere? Think of this exercise as a wardrobe overhaul: Before you set out to shop for new things, get rid of the things that don't look good on you. List twenty-five things you want to toss out of your life. You may find it helpful to look back over the work you've done so far for some helpful reminders.

1. ....

2. ....

3. ....

4. ....

5. ....

6. ....

7. ....

8. ....

9. ....

10. ....

11. ....

12. ....

13. ....

14. ....

15. ....

16. ....

17. ....

18. ....

19. ....

20. ....

21. ....

22. ....

23. ....

24. ....

25. ....

SO, WHAT IS IT YOU *REALLY* WANT?

Imagine that I'm a fairy godfather (and not the type from *The Sopranos*) who just arrived from never-never land. You have an opportunity to get what you want most in life, but on one condition: You have to be able to name what you want in such clear terms that I can't mistake what you're after. Be specific about what you want, when you want it, and how you plan to get it! If you don't make it absolutely clear, or if I suspect you're not disclosing the thing, feeling, or state of mind you're really after, I'll disappear in an instant. Warning: Don't confuse an object, event, or activity with the feeling you think that object, event, or activity will give you! By not allowing yourself to become stuck on an object, event, or activity as the focus of what you "want," you give yourself a lot of flexibility. If you are wise enough to realize that what you want are the feelings you think would come from getting a car or being friends with a superstar, then you can find any number of ways to get that feeling. If you are open to different experiences, you may find, for example, that you get real feelings of self-respect and pride from being a good friend rather than from having a superstar friend. Take this opportunity to figure out exactly what it is that you are striving for in life. Before you can ever achieve it, you must first be extremely specific about what it is that you are aiming for.

1. **What do you want?**

....

....

....

2. What must you do to have it?

....

....

....

3. How would you feel when you got it?

....

....

....

4. Now, tell me what you really want again, but use the answer you just gave to question 3. "What I really want is . . . [answer to question 3]":

....

....

....

5. What must you do to have what you really want?

....

....

....

6. How would that make you feel?

....

....

....

7. Now, tell me what you really want again, but use the answer you just gave to question 6. "What I really want is . . . [answer to question 6]":

....

....

....

8. Repeat questions 4 through 7 as many times as necessary until the answer is certain to you.

....

....

....

Now answer these questions, keeping in mind your answer to question 7 above:

1. How will it you look to people other than yourself when you get what you want?
   Describe yourself and your life from their point of view.

....

....

....

2. Will you look different to others? Will you look differently, enter a room differently, etc ... ?

....

....

....

3. How will it make *you* feel about yourself?

....

....

....

4. What kinds of reactions and feelings will it generate in other people?

....

....

....

5. What time of year is it?

....

6. Who are you with?

....

7. Where are you?

....

8. What are you wearing?

....

9. How old are you?

....

When you can accurately and specifically visualize what it will be like when you have exactly what you want, you will have taken a huge step toward actually getting it!

WHAT STANDS IN MY WAY RIGHT NOW?

Imagine yourself as a cop running after dangerous criminals who have busted out of prison and are preying upon the townspeople. You have cast your net far and wide in order to catch these menaces to society. Imagine the criminals are all of your negative behaviors and emotions out on the loose, wrecking your life. Go back through all of the previous exercises to find and catch all of these little menaces—attitudes, personality traits, habits, tendencies, etc.—and drag them into the light. They are your worst enemies and their only goal is to stop you from getting what you want and need in life. Acknowledge that they are obstacles and that you want to overcome them. Shine your flashlight in their faces. Check off any of the following that have a history of tripping you up and add more of your own.

_____ your comfort zone–remember, this is your routine, your same old day-to-day

_____ shyness

_____ your tendency to judge others

_____ insecurity

_____ jealousy

_____ negative tapes–those mean or destructive things you tell yourself

_____ guilt

_____ the feeling that you are a victim

_____ lousy excuses

_____ dishonesty

____ self-consciousness

____ bitterness

____ self-destructive behavior

____ laziness

____ fear of failure

____ low standards

KEEP GOING!!

....

....

....

....

MARCHING ORDERS FOR SUCCESS

Think of this as your big send-off into the world of limitless possibilities. If you were a secret agent on a complex mission, you would be given a list of orders to complete specific tasks. You might be told not to consider the mission complete until you have carried out all of the orders. Imagine that your spy captain has issued you marching orders for the most important mission you've ever undertaken: improving your life. What must you be mindful of as you proceed on this mission? What important pieces of guidance or advice must you carry with you at all times? Come up with an asterisked list that includes all your essential orders. What will it look like? Here's mine:

★ Stay on task. Don't get distracted.

★ Organize your time so you can get the job done.

★ Take a little time each week to review your progress.

★ Set one mini-goal a week and make it happen.

★ Set aside time to relax, reflect, and refresh yourself.

★ Enlist as much help as possible.

You get the picture. Now make a list of your own. Keep it where you will see it every day.

★ ....

★ ....

★ ....

★ ....

★ ....

★ ....

★ ....

★ ....

★ ....

★ ....

You're about to enter a really exciting stage of your life. You are now in possession of not only the raw materials to make your life what you want it to be, but also the insight, perspectives, and guidance to make the changes you need to make. So want it and act on it! Do yourself the biggest favor of your life. You are, right now, more prepared than you have ever been to go out and get the things that you want in your life. Take advantage of this opportunity because you have earned it!

PART III

GET READY

THE TEN LIFE LAWS MADE SIMPLE: A REFERENCE

N O MATTER HOW SUCCESSFUL OR ACCOMPLISHED A PERSON becomes, at one point or another everyone doubts themselves, their worth, or their value. So, no matter how lonely, discouraged, insecure, or unhappy you feel at any given time, you are not alone—far from it.

Just remember what I said in the conclusion of *Life Strategies for Teens:* There never, ever in the history of the world has been and never, ever in the future of the world will be another you. You are an original. What a sorry waste it would be if you never let yourself *be* that unique person because you were so busy trying to impress or be accepted by someone else, or you were caught up in fighting the authority figures in your life. Don't be so focused on the ultimately unimportant things in life that you forget about being who you really are. Good luck and "go get 'em!" You have to work hard to prepare yourself to succeed and I know you will. Now go have some fun!

You have the only one of you, so treat yourself as the treasure you really are. Believe in who *you* are and don't compare yourself to other people, which is just a waste of time. You have the potential for a great life ahead of you, but it is up to you to live it.

Here are the Ten Life Laws reduced to their most basic principles. Whenever you need a little reality check, guidance, or encouragement, turn to these simple truths. They won't fail you.

LIFE LAW #1

YOU EITHER GET IT, OR YOU DON'T

You can choose to be one who "gets it."

The world works as a system: If you learn that system, you will have an advantage over everybody else.

It is not uncool to want a better life and work toward getting one.

Learning and using the life laws will help you become one who "gets it."

LIFE LAW #2

YOU CREATE YOUR OWN EXPERIENCE

You choose the statement you make to the world with your attitude and appearance. When you choose that statement, you choose how the world will respond to you.

If you don't like the way people treat you, you can change that by changing the statement you make to them.

What role do you play? Is it getting you the results that you want?

You, and you alone, are responsible for the experiences you have in life.

LIFE LAW #3

PEOPLE DO WHAT WORKS

If you are continually doing something that you don't like, you *are* doing it for a reason.

Until you figure out *why* you do the things that you don't like, you will never stop doing them.

If people are treating you in a way that you don't like, find out what their payoff is and eliminate it. If you do, they *will* change their approach to you.

Ignoring the payoffs of your own negative behavior will cost you in the long run.

LIFE LAW #4

YOU CANNOT CHANGE WHAT YOU DO NOT ACKNOWLEDGE

If you don't acknowledge that something is bothering you, it will never change.

Don't spoil your chances for success by denying your problems.

Peer pressure may be an issue that you need to acknowledge and deal with.

It is often easy but less rewarding to stay in a comfort zone. Break out of that comfort zone and you will be rewarded for it.

LIFE REWARDS ACTION

Be, do, have. If you do nothing, you will have nothing.

Take action today so that you don't miss your window of opportunity.

Make a decision to take reasonable, responsible risks. If you never try, you will never succeed.

Don't give up if you don't succeed immediately. Eventually you will succeed.

THERE IS NO REALITY, ONLY PERCEPTION

Your emotions are based on your perception of what is happening to you. If you perceive something as scary, then to you it is scary.

Your perceptions of the world are based on the lenses through which you see things. You can, however, change your lenses.

Don't be influenced by your personal tapes. Evaluate everything based on what is currently happening.

You are the only person who can change your perception of yourself and your life.

LIFE IS MANAGED; IT IS NOT CURED

You will encounter problems for the rest of your life, but there will be nothing you can't manage.

You are your own life manager, and successful management is an acquired skill.

Replace short-term willpower with a long-term program.

Put your life management on project status.

Develop a specific goal plan and you *will* be successful.

WE TEACH PEOPLE HOW TO TREAT US

People "size you up" based on how you present yourself to the world.

People test you to see how you will allow them to treat you.

You can control your life by working within the boundaries by which you are limited. You can retrain people to treat you better.

Treat yourself well so that others will be motivated to do the same.

LIFE LAW #9

THERE IS POWER IN FORGIVENESS

Realize that emotional wounds scar like physical wounds.

Remember that withdrawing emotionally can affect you physically.

Holding on to previous hurts poisons all potential relationships.

Forgiveness is a choice that you are entitled to.

No matter who you are, you are worth it.

LIFE LAW #10

YOU HAVE TO NAME IT BEFORE YOU CAN CLAIM IT

You must be able to describe specifically what it is that you want.

Winners in life know exactly what they want. Do you?

Don't confuse wanting an object or an event with the feelings that come with that object or event.

If you don't know exactly what you want, you can't know if what you are doing is moving you closer to, or further away from, your finish line.

Be prepared to step up and claim the things that you want. They are there to be taken only because you have worked to put them there.

YOU *CAN* BE A WINNER: THE CHOICE IS YOURS.

ABOUT THE AUTHOR

JAY MCGRAW grew up in Dallas, Texas. He is currently a student at the University of Texas at Austin. Jay enjoys spending time with his girlfriend, Jennifer, and his younger brother, Jordan. Playing basketball, piloting small planes, and scuba diving are his favorite hobbies.

Also available...

from the *New York Times* bestselling author
Jay McGraw

The first guide to teenage life that won't tell you what to do, or who to be, but rather how to live life best!

0-7432-1546-X • $14.00